CW00383440

HEADSTART HISTORY

Spain and 1492:
Unity and Uniformity
under Ferdinand and Isabella

by

David Abulafia

HEADSTART HISTORY

Published by   HEADSTART HISTORY
                    PO Box 41, Bangor, Gwynedd, LL57 1SB

Set by   C.B.S.
                    155 Hamilton Road,
                    Felixstowe, Suffolk, IP11 7DR

Printed by   Henry Ling Ltd.,
                    The Dorset Press,
                    Dorchester
                    DT1 1HD

ISBN   1 873041 21 7

A CIP catalogue record for this book is available from the British Library.

For Bianca and Rosa

Cuando el Rey Nimrod al campo salía
mirava en el cielo y en l'estreyería.
Vidó luz santa en la judería
que havia de nacer Avraham avinu...

Ladino song

ACKNOWLEDGMENTS

My sincere thanks are due to Cecilia Cordeiro Engels and Stefan Smith for doing so much to stimulate my thoughts about the *conversos* and about Atlantic exploration, respectively.

Anna Sapir Abulafia and Stephan Epstein were kind enough to read the text and make invaluable comments. I am also grateful to Mark Meyerson whose ideas, in word and print, I have found most stimulating.

CONTENTS

Cover illustrations: Isabella of Castile
and Ferdinand of Aragon
Artist unknown

Acknowledgements: and thanks for the use of portraits in the
Royal Collection which are reproduced
by gracious permission of
H.M. the Queen.

INTRODUCTION

The HEADSTART HISTORY PAPERS aim to identify important themes and topics the significance of which extends beyond the studies of professional historians. The PAPERS are distillations of the research of distinguished scholars in a form appropriate to students and the general reader.

In his log book for 1492 Christopher Columbus noted three important events in the history of Spain. At the beginning of that year Ferdinand and Isabella had led their victorious army into Granada thus ending nearly 800 years of Muslim rule in the Iberian peninsula. Less than three months later a decree went out from the court giving Jews a choice of conversion to Christianity or enforced exile from their ancestral land. Finally Columbus wrote that the monarchs had decided to send him:-

> 'to see those parts of India and the princes and people of those lands and consider the best means for their conversion.'

David Abulafia gives us a lucid exposition of the political developments in Spain following the marriage of Ferdinand and Isabella : examines the religious tensions between the Christian monarchy and their Jewish and Muslim subjects and how those problems were increased with the expansion of the Spanish Empire. But this PAPER is unique in so far as the author has a strong personal link with the subject on which he writes - his ancestors appear in the text since they were expelled with others of their faith when the decree required Jews to conform or leave. In a lighter vein, a hero in the historical novel *The Source* by James Michener is a Marrano named 'Dr Abulafia'!

David Abulafia is a Fellow of Gonville and Caius College,

Cambridge and Reader in Mediterranean History in the University of Cambridge, and his numerous writings over the last twenty years reflect not simply his interest in Spain or Italy but in seeing them as Mediterranean lands with trading and political activities based on that area.

This is the first Headstart History Paper to be published in 1992, four hundred years after the events discussed in the pages.

Like the PAPERS by Professor Thody and Dr Bridgham, *Spain and 1492* will appear in translation later in the year to mark HEADSTART'S interest in closer integration with Europe.

I am grateful to David Abulafia for agreeing to write this paper and thus providing readers with a piece which is both elegant in its expression and lucid in its exposition. I wish to thank him as editor of the *JOURNAL OF MEDIEVAL HISTORY* for his swift and generous support to me as proprietor and editor of *Medieval History*. It is a pleasure to acknowledge his help in writing for my journal and in this instance for adding his scholarship to a distinguished series.

Judith Loades
Bangor 1991.

1492: unity and uniformity in fifteenth-century Spain

At the end of March 1492 a decree went out from the court in Granada of Ferdinand and Isabella, rulers of Castile and Aragon, giving the Jews of Spain the choice between conversion to Christianity and forced emigration from their ancestral land. Less than three months earlier, in a campaign that had been partly financed by Jewish supporters of the crown, the victorious armies of Ferdinand and Isabella, with the monarchs at their head, had processed into the city of Granada, the last major Muslim stronghold in Spain, and put to an end seven hundred and eighty-one years of continuous rule by Muslims over parts (at times most) of the Iberian peninsula. The same year, a Genoese sailor imbued with the certainty that he could find a quick route to India and its fabled wealth, voyaged westwards and discovered the eastern fringes of the Caribbean archipelagoes. Christopher Columbus, too, had received some help from financiers of Jewish origin, and he was sailing in the service of the same 'Catholic Monarchs' from Spain.[1] His logbook recorded the three major events of that year, and assumed a link between them: the king and queen 'decided to send me, Christopher Columbus, to see those parts of India and the princes and peoples of those lands, and consider the best means for their conversion.' Hav-

1 The title *Reges Catholici* or *Reyes Católicos*, often translated 'Catholic Kings', was conferred on Ferdinand and Isabella by Pope Alexander VI in 1494 in recognition of such attainments as the conquest of Granada. As is customary, it is used here (though in the form 'Catholic Monarchs') as a convenient shorthand description for the king and queen both before and after 1494.

ing decided to expel the Jews, Columbus goes on to say, the rulers commissioned his voyage to India.

At the same time, then, that the Christians in Spain apparently put to an end the religious diversity that had characterised the peninsula since the early Middle Ages, they were making their first contact with Amerindian peoples in the far west who knew nothing of Christianity. Spanish Christianity thus ended one chapter in the history of its relationship with non-Christians at the exact moment when it began an entirely new chapter in that history. Even so, the break from the past within the Iberian peninsula was not total. As will be seen, the Muslims of Granada were initially granted limited guarantees of the right to worship according to their religion; even though these were set aside after a mere ten years, many Muslims continued the secret practice of Islam under the pretence of being good Catholics, while in the region of Valencia the free practice of Islam continued until 1525. The Moriscos, as the crypto-Muslims are generally known, were only expelled in the early seventeenth century, though until then they were constantly subject to investigation by the Inquisition. The fate of those Jews who remained in Spain was strikingly similar, especially after the Jews of the smaller Iberian kingdoms of Portugal and Navarre were also forced to convert or emigrate in 1497 and 1498. They had been coerced into accepting baptism, some going to the font more eagerly than others. Many continued to practise a form of Judaism, or at least to observe some Jewish practices, for several generations.

In what way were the three major events of 1492 linked?

What is the relationship between them and the wider changes that were taking place in the Iberian peninsula at this time? This is the period when historians identify the coming together of the major Iberian kingdoms, Castile and Aragon, into what was in effect a single unit, though with separate administrations, with Castile assumed to be very obviously in command. It is important, therefore, to begin with some thoughts about the nature of the Spanish kingdoms at the time of the marriage of the Aragonese prince Ferdinand to the Castilian princess Isabella in 1469.

I. Castile and Aragon in the fifteenth century

Conventional wisdom, encapsulated in the study by J.H. Elliott on *Imperial Spain, 1469-1716*, has it that Castile was manifestly the strongest power in the peninsula by the middle or the fifteenth century.[2] Discounting little Navarre, the shrinking Muslim state of Granada, and impoverished but ambitious Portugal, the competition for hegemony was only really open to Castile and Aragon. It had been a real competition, with King Peter IV, 'the Ceremonious', of Aragon seeking to take advantage of civil strife in Castile in the 1360s in order to grab neighbouring pieces of Castile.

Yet Castile and Aragon were often able to collaborate in

---

2 J.H. Elliott, *Imperial Spain 1469-1716* (London, 1963); a similar approach is made explicit by the subtitle of J.N. Hillgarth, *The Spanish Kingdoms*, vol. 2, *Castillian Hegemony, 1410-1516* (Oxford, 1978), which is actually the work of a scholar with a particular interest in the Crown of Aragon.

common objectives such as the conquest of Muslim Murcia (1265) or the clearance of the seas to the east of Gibraltar of Muslim fleets in the 1340s. This was because their major interests were quite different. Aragon proper consisted of a small upland kingdom whose population still included Moors and Jews in the fifteenth century, but was eighty per cent composed of Christians who spoke a language distinct from but not very remote from that of Castile. Under the same king lay the maritime principality of Catalonia, which stretched across the Pyrenees to include Perpignan, an important business centre in what is now southern France. Barcelona was the capital of this Catalan-speaking region, whose inhabitants were very conscious of the linguistic and cultural divide from both Aragon proper and Castile. Further south, the kingdom of Valencia, with its large Moorish population, and the kingdom of Majorca, an important industrial and commercial centre, also formed part of the multiple dominions of the king of Aragon. Moreover, by 1400 their authority extended far beyond Spain. After they conquered Sicily in 1282, the island passed to a cadet line of the Aragonese dynasty; but by the end of the fourteenth century it was reunited to the Crown of Aragon. Sicily was a valuable asset since it was the source of plentiful grain supplies. Historians have pointed to a statement of King Peter IV of Aragon that seems to encapsulate Aragonese policy in the Mediterranean in the late fourteenth and fifteenth centuries:

> If Sardinia is lost, Majorca, without its food supply from Sicily and Sardinia, will be depopulated and will be lost, and Barcelona will also be depopulated, for Barcelona could not

live without Sicily and Sardinia, nor could its
merchants trade if the isles were lost.

Sardinia was also a source of silver, coral and other
valuable products, but it proved extremely hard to conquer; a long delayed invasion began in 1323, but by the
start of the fifteenth century the rebellious petty kings of
Arborea, in the centre of the island, had forced Aragonese
power back to a few strongly defended corners of the
island such as Cagliari and the silver mines of Iglesias in
the south, and the resettled town of Alghero in the north-
west, where to this day the population speaks the Catalan of their settler ancestors.

The major advance in Aragonese power in the fifteenth
century was far away from Spain. Aragon's rulers reaf-
firmed their interest in wider Mediterranean politics when
King Alfonso V of Aragon laid claim in the 1440s to the
kingdom of Naples, a large area of southern Italy which
had originally been attached to the kingdom of Sicily
but which had not fallen to Aragon with the island of
Sicily in 1282, and which still, confusingly, called itself
'the kingdom of Sicily.'[3] Acquiring southern Italy in the
face of stiff opposition from the French prince René,
Duke of Anjou, Alfonso treated it as a springboard for
more ambitious schemes in northern Italy, the Balkans
and even the eastern Mediterranean. All this cost a for-

---

3 For Alfonso, see Alan Ryder, *Alfonso the Magnanimous* (Oxford,
1990); Alan Ryder, *The Kingdom of Naples under Alfonso the
Magnanimous* (Oxford, 1975). For a relatively positive view of
Aragonese finances, see W. Küchler, *Die Finanzen der Krone Aragon
während des 15. Jahrhunderts (Alfons V. und Johann II)*, (Münster,
1983).

tune, which Alfonso was ruthless in raising by heavy taxation, the sale of offices, loans from bankers; he sold the city of Cefalù in Sicily to a new master even though it was supposed to be free in perpetuity, and he sold one beneficiary some lands in Sicily on the express condition that even if he sold them again to someone else they were in fact the property of the original beneficiary. At one point before his death in 1458 it looked as if the whole of Italy, notably the Duchy of Milan, would be his, and a new Roman Empire seemed on the verge of creation. Pompous medals and grandiose sculptures, such as the beautiful triumphal arch which still exists in Naples, portrayed Alfonso as the equal of the ancient Caesars.[4]

This led to the neglect of Spanish affairs; Aragon, Catalonia and Valencia were governed on his behalf by viceroys, a system that worked most effectively when they were members of the royal family, such as his estranged queen. But there were severe social tensions within Catalonia which were in danger of being overlooked. Part of the peasantry remained unfree, subject to what were described as *mals usos*, bad usages, imposed by landlords anxious to draw on the large labour reserve the peasants offered.[5] Obligatory labour services to landlords were especially attractive at a time when Europe's population was continuing to suffer devastating outbreaks of plague; rural labour was in short supply as a result of the mortality, and wage labourers were more expensive than they

---

4 Jerry Bentley, *Politics and Culture in Renaissance Naples* (Princeton, NJ, 1987).

5 Paul Freedman, *The origins of peasant servitude in medieval Catalonia* (Cambridge, 1991).

had been before the Black Death. However, the unfree (or *remença*) peasants agitated for release; many were actually quite well off, and therefore felt the humiliation of their status all the more. Offers of money to Alfonso and his queen were remarkably successful. The monarchy was well disposed to the peasants, especially if they could produce so much urgently needed cash. But unfortunately the parliament of Catalonia, the *Corts*, representing in part the noble opposition to these peasants, forced the monarchy to withdraw its support for the unfree peasants. The problem was left unresolved, and when civil war broke out in Catalonia in 1462, the *remences* were in the front line.

In the cities too there were signs of crisis. A populist faction in Barcelona, the *Busca*, gained royal support in its attempts to unseat the old patrician *Biga*. The *Busca* had a radical programme of economic reform, or *redreç*, aimed at problems such as the money supply (there were serious shortages of good bullion as a result of unrealistic official exchange rates for gold and silver in Barcelona).[6] The city banks had been in crisis since the 1380s, and even the creation of a public credit institution in 1401, the *Taula de Canvi,* (pronounced 'Cambi'; meaning 'Table of Exchange') had not restored faith in public finances, though it was given control over the city budget.[7] In the mid-fifteenth century social conflicts also affected another major centre of Aragonese economic power, the

---

6 C. Batlle Gallart, *La crisis social y ecónomica de Barcelona a mediados del siglo XV, 2 vols* (Barcelona, 1973).

7 A.P. Usher. *The early history of deposit banking in Mediterranean Europe* (Cambridge, MA, 1943), 269-77.

City of Majorca (modern Palma).[8]

The traditional picture is thus a rather gloomy one of the once great Catalan trading network, which had dominated the western Mediterranean around 1300, now in steep decline. This is not, however, so widely believed nowadays. Barcelona's population plummeted in the late fifteenth century, to about 75,000 in 1483, but this was at the end of a trying period of civil war. Until the 1470s the keynote of Catalan economic life was crisis rather than decline. When Alfonso of Aragon conquered Naples in the 1440s he did so in the face of tough Florentine opposition; the Florentines had a strong hold on the economy of Naples. They were mostly kicked out, and it is striking how rapidly and successfully the Catalans filled the gap, becoming within very few years the largest group of foreign merchants in the city, and completely dominating its textile trade for many years; they also traded intensively to Palermo, in Sicily, Alghero, in Sardinia, and to areas outside the Aragonese political orbit such as Rhodes. Some historians, such as the eminent Italian scholar Mario del Treppo, have argued that Alfonso was seeking to create a western Mediterranean 'Common Market' in the lands he ruled.[9] After he died, southern

---

8 Hillgarth, Spanish Kingdoms, ii.80.

9 M. del Treppo, *I mercanti catalani e l'espansione della Corona d'Aragona nel secolo XV* (Naples, 1972); cf. C. Carrère, *Barcelone centre économique à l'époque des difficultés 1380-1462*, 2 vols (Paris/The Hague, 1967), which points part of the way in the same direction. The old approach of P. Vilar, 'Le déclin catalan au bas Moyen Age,' *Estudios de Historia moderna,* vi (1956-9), 1-68, dominates Elliott, *Imperial Spain,* 24-30, but cannot now be accepted.

Italy was separated from the other Aragonese lands and was made over to his illegitimate son Ferrante, or Ferdinand, I of Naples; Ferrante was, however, considered one of the family, and in 1480-1 the Turkish occupation of Otranto, in Ferrante's kingdom, elicited a decisive response from Spain in the form of a Castilian and Aragonese fleet. The presence of Catalan merchants and cloths in Italy remained very significant too; Minorca became a major wool exporter by 1400, supplying the famous Tuscan merchant Francesco Datini, the 'merchant of Prato', with large amounts of wool; and Majorcan cloths made from Minorcan and other wools were in sound demand. It was only with the civil war of 1462-72 that a sharp decline set in, as Barcelona was incapacitated; even so, recent studies suggest that the merchants bounced back once the war was over.[10] Barcelona did not collapse; maybe it did not even decline; but it experienced lengthy crises and, during the civil war, severe recession.

The question of the 'decline' of Catalonia can be addressed from another angle. It is true that the once frequent sailings of Catalan and Majorcan ships to Flanders and England came to an effective end by the mid-fifteenth century. The other side of the coin is the increasing interest of Catalan cloth makers in English wool, brought in mainly on Italian ships. This new supply did much to stimulate the city's economy in the mid-fifteenth century. What had happened was, first, that the Italians and other foreign merchants had come to domi-

---

10 M. Peláez, *Catalunya desprès de la guerra civil del segle XV* (Barcelona, 1981).

nate the long distance sailings into the Atlantic; but secondly the ships that passed through Aragonese waters were now visiting a more conveniently situated port than Barcelona: Valencia. Here there was a veritable economic boom in the fifteenth century.[11] In 1483 it may have had four times the population of Barcelona, though this is clearly an extreme contrast taken from Barcelona's worst years. Valencia was itself a source or rice, dried fruits and other luxuries typical of the Islamic world, many of which were less easily accessible elsewhere than they had been before because of the Turkish advances in the eastern Mediterranean. Their availability in Spain brought Flemish, German, Milanese, Venetian and other merchants to Valencia.[12] Another attraction was the magnificent 'Hispano-Moresque' pottery made to order in the area around Valencia for the nobility of Europe. So too the excellent quality of the gold currency of Valencia in the mid-fifteenth century provides a curious contrast to the position in Barcelona, and serves as a reminder that the political and economic integration of these lands into a single Aragonese whole was neither achieved nor desired. Valencia, Aragon and Catalonia had their own separate coinages, as they had their own separate parliaments and laws.[13]

---

11 J. Guiral-Hadziiossif, *Valence, port méditerranéen au XVe siècle (1410-1525)* (Paris, 1986); A.Furió (ed.), *València, un mercat medieval* (Valencia, 1985).

12 P. Mainoni, *Mercanti lombardi fra Barcellona e Valenza nel basso medioevo* (Milan, 1983), partially reprinted in Furió, *València,* 81-156.

13 E. Hamilton, *Money, prices and wages in Valencia, Aragon and Navarre, 1351-1500* (Cambridge, MA, 1936).

The lack of resources of the monarchs made them increasingly reliant on votes of funds from the parliaments; a 'pactist' view of royal power emerged, which the monarchy found it hard to resist, according to which the king was in a contractual relationship with his subjects, and if he failed to respect their rights they could have recourse to their last and greatest right, that of denying the authority of the crown.[14] The dangers to the crown were seen in the civil war of 1462-72, a messy series of conflicts that involved the peasants, the towns, the *Corts* and even the king of France, Louis XI, who invaded the Catalan counties on the French side of the Pyrenees and supported the claims of the French duke René of Anjou to the throne of Aragon.[15] Ferdinand's marriage to Isabella thus came at a time when the ruling house of Aragon needed all the allies it could find against powerful external and internal foes.

Castile presents a very different profile. Although the king was able to make use of a list of royal titles (king of Toledo, Murcia, Córdoba, Seville, and so on) far longer than that in Aragon, the reality was that the great assortment of lands he ruled had been integrated into a single whole for administrative purposes; there was no scattered overseas empire to dissipate royal resources and attention, though ambitions in Morocco and even (for one bizarre moment) Germany are documented. The monarchy was able to escape the threat of pactism by

---

14 Hillgarth, *Spanish Kingdoms,* ii.203-5, 247-8.

15 J. Calmette, *Louis XI, Jean II et la révolution catalane (1461-1473)* (Toulouse, 1903); Hillgarth, *Spanish Kingdoms,* ii.267-99.

appealing to Roman law and to the image of the ruler as an autocrat whose will was the source of law. The *Cortes* or parliament of Castile was carefully circumscribed; to a large extent its membership consisted of representatives of the towns, in which, especially under the Catholic Monarchs, royal power was decisively asserted through the appointment of city governors. The *Cortes* could not try to speak with one voice as the representative of all Castile. Equally, noble power, especially in far-flung regions such as Extremadura, was formidable. The late fourteenth and fifteenth centuries saw a series of attempts to rein in the power of the nobles; the battle was far from won when Ferdinand and Isabella married. To some extent, it has to be admitted, the nobles tolerated the pretensions of the monarchy because they suffered so little from the realisation of those pretensions. On the other hand, the nobles could be quite ruthless in exploiting divisions in the royal house. The civil war between Pedro the Cruel (d.1369) and his illegitimate half-brother Henry of Trastámara, which had serious repercussions for the Jewish communities of Castile, played into the hands of those nobles who resented Pedro's attempts to recover lost taxes and restore royal finances. The fifteenth century reads as a catalogue of rebellions and grievances, against the controversial, supposedly dissolute, Henry IV, and finally against the claims of queen Isabella herself. The real mystery is why historians assume Castile was stronger than Aragon. Its rulers may have claimed more powers; whether they could exercise those powers is another matter. Another point that has tended to be forgotten is that the royal house of Aragon exercised considerable influence in fifteenth-century Castile well before Ferdinand of Aragon became the husband of the Castilian queen. In 1410 the house of Barcelona had died out and the nobles of the Crown of Aragon chose as successor a Castilian prince related to their former rulers, Ferdinand of Antequera. He and his son Alfonso V (1416-58) controlled extensive lands in Castile, and for a time it seemed these kings of Aragon would have a decisive voice in its future.[16]

Thus the unity of Castile must not be exaggerated. It was larger than Aragon, but its population was more spread out; it is far from clear, in any case, that size of population was sufficient to determine its greater success, and it is regrettable that so much has been made of this factor (including the questionable use of sixteenth-century statistics to prove the point for the fifteenth century).[17] In any case, a proper measurement of Aragon would include the Italian lands as well. The one obvious way in which a large Castilian population could strengthen the crown was in providing larger revenues, but local disaffection and the problem of controlling remote regions of Spain meant that this was less of an advantage than it might seem. Apart from Segovia, there were no major industrial centres in the fifteenth century. Castile's strength lay in wool production, which since the late thirteenth century had been organised through the *Mesta*, a massive sheep guild that eventually fell under the control of several noble families.[18] (In addition, some

---

16 Ryder, *Alfonso*, 116-74.

17 Elliott, *Imperial Spain*, 13, is unacceptable.

18 J. Klein, *The Mesta: a study in Spanish economic history 1273-1836* (Cambridge, MA, 1920).

areas in the south-west were given over to cattle raising, and it has been argued that it was in the late medieval Extremadura that the supposedly American institutions of the cowboy and the rodeo originated).[19] The seasonal movement of sheep from high to low ground between winter and summer demanded prodigious powers of organisation, since it intruded on land rights. However, the best cloth made from this wool was made outside Castile, in Catalonia, Majorca, Florence, Flanders. Where Castile benefited was in the acquisition of large amounts of gold and silver in payment for the country's wools. The result was that the bullion shortages which so affected the prosperity of Catalonia were just about avoided, the more so since the monarchy took an intelligent interest in the bullion problem.[20]

In the period from about 1250 onwards Castile began to emerge as a significant naval power. There were several reasons for this. One was the growing market for Spanish produce, such as metals and of course wool, in northern Europe; Castilian merchants became a familiar sight in London even before 1300.[21] Another was the opening of regular sea trade routes from Italy, Majorca and Catalonia to England and Flanders around 1277. The ports of Cantabria and the Basque country, ranged in a line along

---

19 J. Bishko, *Studies in medieval Spanish frontier history* (London, 1980).

20 A. Mackay, *Money, prices and politics in fifteenth-century Castile* (London, 1981).

21 W. Childs, *Anglo-Castilian trade in the later Middle Ages* (Manchester, 1978).

the southern fringe of the Bay of Biscay, responded vigorously; in the fifteenth century a league of the Cantabrian maritime towns, the *Hermandad de las Marismas*, was able to coordinate and protect the sea trade northwards in Castilian wool.[22] Further east, the Basque fishermen had already developed navigational skills that enabled them to sail in poor weather out of sight of land. Now they moved south to Seville, which had been conquered by the king of Castile in 1248, and they acted as intermediaries on the sea routes tying the Mediterranean to the Atlantic.[23] Catalan or Italian shippers would cooperate with Basque sailors on the route to the North Sea. Moreover, the attractive produce of southern Spain, exotic fruits, wine, pottery, good quality grain, were in growing demand in the late fourteenth century; Christian Andalucia, inhabited largely by a settler population of Christian conquerors and their descendants, had a very distinct economic character from northern Castile. It is noticeable that Valencia and Seville responded to similar stimuli; neither Castile nor Aragon was the exclusive beneficiary of the important economic changes that were taking place.

It was the Italians, rather than native Spaniards, who were the crucial factor in the development of Castile's maritime power. The Genoese set up a major trading

---

22 H. Kamen, *Spain 1469-1714. A society of conflict* (2nd ed., London, 1991), 13.

23 J. Heers, 'Le commerce des Basques en Méditerranée au XVe siècle,' *Bulletin hispanique,* lvii (1955), 292-324, repr. in J. Heers, *Société et économie à Gênes (XIVe-XVe siècles)* (London, 1979).

base in Seville after the routes to the Atlantic were opened up, but they were already a powerful presence long before.[24] They also acted, with the great Florentine banks, as a major financial support to the crown. A similar picture, on a smaller scale, obtains for Portugal in this period.[25] All this was in stark contrast to Barcelona, where big business had been dominated by native Catalan merchants, Christian or Jewish, and where foreigners were rigorously excluded, especially bankers from Italy. The links were strengthened by the presence of Genoese admirals in the Castilian fleet during the fourteenth century. The Castilians went out to buy the best captains available from Genoa, as, in the same period, did the French; the Basque sailors apart, Castile lacked a maritime tradition in any way comparable to that of Catalonia and Majorca, but it compensated for this by heavy investment in war fleets.

One problem in the existing literature on the Spain of Ferdinand and Isabella is the sheer assumption that Spain's destiny lay with Castile. The terms of the marriage alliance between Ferdinand and Isabella (1469) are seen as humiliating to Aragon, as in some sense they were; but they reflect a state of affairs where neither party to the marriage was universally recognised as future monarch, and where it was important for Isabella to be able to call on the resources of Aragon to defend her against her rival Juana, and for Ferdinand to have support against

---

24 R. Pike, *Enterprise and adventure. The Genoese in Seville and the opening of the New World* (Icatha, NY, 1966).

25 B. Diffie, *Prelude to Empire. Portugal overseas before Henry the Navigator* (Nebraska, 1960).

the French pretender René of Anjou; even King Henry IV of Castile was unhappy about the Aragonese marriage. Thus Ferdinand was to spend his time mainly in Castile and he was only to reign as co-ruler in Isabella's lifetime.[26] Another side to these stipulations was surely the fear that Aragon would lord it over Castile. No one was in a position to say that Catalonia's once strong economy was in irredeemable decline; its Mediterranean empire remained intact, and the social tensions that afflicted Barcelona, Majorca, Sicily were not completely absent in Castile, as will be plain when the status of the Jews comes under examination. Ferdinand was of Castilian descent, and the memory of the Antequera hegemony in Castile in the early fifteenth century was still fresh; the brother of Alfonso of Aragon had acquired the crown of Navarre, thereby boxing in Castile on its Pyrenean frontier (admittedly he did little to serve Aragon's wider interests thereafter, until he became king of Aragon and surrendered Navarre). The conclusion seems to be that the marriage was a good proposition for Aragon, even though it perpetuated the tendency of the Aragonese kings to reside outside their core territories; for Castile, or rather the would-be heiress Isabella, it was a straw at which to clutch in the hope of making real a claim to the crown that, in 1469, not all the nobles of Castile were prepared to countenance. Even after King Henry died in 1474, it took some years to convince the Castilian grandees that Isabella's claims were irresistible.

Both kingdoms were evidently in need of reconstruction after Ferdinand and Isabella saw off their enemies in the

---

26 Elliott, *Imperial Spain*, 6-12, 30-2; Kamen, *Spain*, 1, 9-10

1470's. What is noteworthy is the great conservatism of Ferdinand's policies in Aragon. In 1480-1 he confirmed the traditional powers of the Catalan *Corts* and its permanent committees; even when, in 1494, he put together a Council of Aragon for the whole group of kingdoms that made up the Crown of Aragon, he was only returning to methods that had been laid down by Alfonso the Magnanimous in the 1440's.[27] In freeing the *remença* peasants, with the *Sentencia de Guadalupe* of 1486, he was merely doing what earlier kings had promised to do. Ferdinand had no intention whatsoever of suppressing the traditional liberties of the Catalans and of imposing Castilian hegemony over Aragon.[28] In Castile, reconstruction followed more innovative lines, for the assertion of royal authority seemed easier. The towns became the lever for the extension of crown power through much of the kingdom. The monarchy took control of the *hermandades* (literally, 'brotherhoods'), town councils with police powers, using them between 1476 and 1498 to restore order, often by imposing stiff penalties on law breakers.[29] Subsequently the *corregidores* emerged as the key link between the crown and the towns; these officials combined administrative and judicial duties; government supervision of these powerful officials, and the

---

27 Alan Ryder, 'The evolution of imperial government in Naples under Alfonso V,' in J.R. Hale, J.R.L. Highfield, B. Smalley (eds) *Europe in the late Middle Ages* (London, 1965), 332-57, a point not sufficiently appreciated by Elliott, *Imperial Spain,* 71-2.

28 Elliott, *Imperial Spain,* 70.

29 M. Lunenfeld, *The Council of the Santa Hermandad* (Miami, 1970); Kamen, *Spain,* 17-19.

increasing insistence of the crown on the primacy of its own courts, meant that by the early sixteenth century the Castilian monarchy had gained enormously in authority throughout the kingdom.[30] The *corregidores* were themselves supervised by a central *Consejo Real*, Royal Council, in which the monarchs took care to place professional administrators, including converted Jews trained in the law; the old nobility had some access to the Council, but was not allowed to dominate it. The powerful Military Orders, religious institutions which were well endowed with land, were brought out of the hands of the nobility and under royal control; between 1476 and 1494 the Grand Masterships of the orders of Santiago, Calatrava and Alcántara were acquired by Ferdinand.[31] Although, as in Aragon, the Catholic Monarchs were building on precedent at least as much as they were innovating, their reorganisation of Castile greatly enhanced royal authority by proving that the Crown could offer peace and stability. If the common assumption that Castile was the stronger kingdom by 1492 be valid, then the explanation must lie more in the reconstruction achieved by Ferdinand and Isabella after 1474 than in any longstanding primacy it had supposedly acquired.

A word should be said about cultural developments in Christian Spain which were common to the courts of

---

30 M. Lunenfeld, *Keepers of the City. The corregidores of Isabella of Castile (1474-1504)* (Cambridge, 1988); for an account of one city, though an atypical one, see J.H. Edwards, *Christian Córdoba. The city and its region in the late Middle Ages* (Cambridge, 1982).

31 Elliott, *Imperial Spain,* 76-7; Kamen, *Spain,* 26-7.

Aragon and Castile during the fifteenth century. There was a revival of interest in the romantic love lyrics which had first been disseminated in twelfth-century Provence and Gascony by the troubadours.[32] This turning back to literary models of a by-gone age was part of a wider insistence on the need to restore traditional chivalric values among the knighthood of Spain. The romantic novel *Tirant lo Blanc,* by Joan Martorell, is a good example of this genre; it is known to have influenced Cervantes in his famous satire on knightly manners, *Don Quixote.*[33] In the novel *Curial and Guelfa* the reader is transported back to the heroic age of Catalan expansion in the Mediterranean, and into a world where valour, strength of arms and other traditional values hold sway.[34] In the same period in Castile there is greater emphasis on the idea of being the son of someone significant, the literal meaning of the term *hidalgo.* Members of Old Christian families wished to assert that they were of unsullied blood, descended from the ancient Gothic rulers of Spain; it is no coincidence that there was an outpouring of ballads about life on the frontier with Muslim Granada, for acts of bravery against the Infidel were a stock-in-trade of the writer of chivalric romances.[35]

---

32 R. Boase, *The Troubadour Revival. A study of social change and traditionalism in late medieval Spain* (London, 1978).

33 D.H. Rosenthal (transl.), *Tirant lo Blanc* (London, 1984).

34 P. Waley (transl.), *Curial and Guelfa* (London, 1982).

35 A. MacKay, 'The ballad and the frontier in late medieval Spain,' *Bulletin of Hispanic Studies,* liii (1976), 15-33, repr. in A. Mackay, *Society, politics and religion in late medieval Castile* (London, 1987).

II. The end of Moorish Spain

The war against the Moors was, then, part of the culture of the fighting and ruling classes in late medieval Spain. Under the impact of the early crusades, in the late eleventh and twelfth centuries, the Spanish reconquista took on the character of a holy war for the recovery of the land stolen from its original Christian rulers by the Muslim invaders of 711.[36] However, by the end of the Middle Ages this war had undergone some important internal transformations. The Nasrid sultanate of Granada of the thirteenth to fifteenth centuries differed from the earlier Muslim states in Spain by being almost entirely Muslim in population, without a significant Christian population. Its rulers aspired not to recover Muslim control throughout Spain but to hold on to their territory at a time when the rest of Muslim Spain had been whittled away by Aragon and Castile. From the 1240s Granada had been conscious of its specifically Islamic identity, and the founders of the Nasrid state had been enthusiastic proponents of the strict Malikite school of Muslim law. Far from being an island of tolerance in a Spain that was fast coming under the control of triumphalist Christian conquerors, Granada was, as Harvey has pointed out, the home of strict Islam.[37] Fear of Christianity became the unifying theme of Granadan politics, and old tribal loyalties, which had been the main focus of loyalty in Mus-

---

36 R.A. Fletcher, 'Reconquest and crusade in Spain c.1050-1150,' *Transactions of the Royal Historical Society,* ser. 5, xxxvii (1987), 31-47.

37 L.P. Harvey, *Islamic Spain 1250-1500* (Chicago, 1991), 31-44.

lim Spain until now, were set aside. The great north African historian of the late fourteenth century, ibn Khaldun, wrote that 'it is understandable that both people of power and influence and also the lower orders should have been united by a common hatred of the Christian king, whom they feared as an enemy of their religion'.[38] Granada was in part a refuge for Muslims who had fled from the conquerors of Córdoba, Seville, Valencia, Murcia during and after the tremendous Christian advances of the thirteenth century.

Granada was also unstable. Its rulers, anxious in general not to fall under the hegemony of the Marinid rulers of Morocco, took pains to play off Castile against Aragon; periods such as the 1360s when the two Kings Peter of Castile and Aragon were at war were an opportunity to cherish. Equally, Castilian rulers could interfere in the fraught politics of Granada, exploiting the factionalism of the royal court there to assert their own influence in the Muslim kingdom. From 1246 onwards the Castilians were very occasionally able to claim tribute payments (parias) from Granada, for instance in the 1370s under Henry II of Castile and Muhammad V of Granada. But there were enough refusals from Granada to pay up to make plain the continuing independence of the sultanate; in 1417 the Granadans exploited the death of their great enemy Ferdinand of Antequera, a Castilian prince who had become king of Aragon, and substituted a gift of one hundred Christian captives for tribute payment; a legend about a sultan who ruled in the 1470's has him say: ''The kings of Granada who used to give tribute are

---

38 Cited by Harvey, *Islamic Spain*, 164.

dead, and the places in Granada where they used to mint the money are now being used to make spear-heads to prevent its being paid again.'' It has now been demonstrated that the traditional view that Granada had become an enfeebled vassal state of Castile two and a half centuries before the final capture of Granada underestimates the capacity of the Muslims to hold off Christian armies and to exploit to their own advantage the constant squabbling between Aragon and Castile.[39] Occasional north African help, mainly in the form of an army of African Volunteers, also counted for much, while the Granadans took advantage of new military technology in the form of the cannon.

A particular strength of the Granadan state was the growing interest of Italian merchants in its produce: dried fruits and other specialised agricultural goods drew Genoese, Florentines and others to Málaga; these goods were transported as far as England and Flanders as well as towards Italy. Fifteenth-century Granada has been seen by the French historian Jacques Heers as an economic colony of the Italian merchants.[40] Their presence helped bolster the sultan's finances; the rulers of Granada seem to demonstrate their solvency through their magnificent building plans, especially the superb Alhambra palace built largely under Muhammad V (d.1391).[41] The Italian

---

39 Harvey, *Islamic Spain,* 191-2, 241-2, 266.

40 J. Heers, 'Le royaume de Grenade et la politique marchande de Gênes en Occident (XVe siècle)', *Le Moyen Age,* lxiii (1957), 87-121, repr. in Heers, *Société et économie;* F. Melis, *I mercanti italiani nell'Europa medievale e rinascimentale* (Florence/Prato, 1990).

41 O. Grabar, *The Alhambra* (London, 1978); G. Goodwin, *Islamic Spain* (London, 1989).

connection shows that the Granadan economy had already turned its back on North Africa and that it had been brought into the trading network of the Christian Mediterranean well before its fall to Castile. This marked a signal victory for the Italians, who had much to fear if Granada renewed its links to the Marinid sultans of Morocco, and threatened to close the Straits of Gibraltar to Christian shipping. In 1449, a desperate attempt by Granada to mobilise Navarre in its support reveals that the Granadans were not alone in knowing that the Castile harboured designs on its smaller neighbours.[42] But such an alliance could never be more than a minor irritant to Castile.

In the late fifteenth century the political configuration changed decisively; the marriage of Ferdinand and Isabella left Granada unable to play off the two Christian kingdoms against each other. Internal divisions within Granada gave Ferdinand a golden opportunity to support a contender for the Granadan throne, Boabdil (also known as Sultan Muhammad XII); Boabdil's assumption of power, followed by his brave attempt to convince the Granadans that he was not a puppet of the Catholic Monarchs, gave Ferdinand his excuse to launch a final campaign. In 1487 a series of campaigns along the Mediterranean coast culminated in the fall of Málaga, the main commercial outlet of Granada, to be followed two years later by the occupation of the other sea port, Almeria.[43] Having stolen control of the coast from the Muslims, the

---

42 Harvey, *Islamic Spain*, 256-7.

43 Harvey, *Islamic Spain*, 275-308.

Christians had bottled up Boabdil in Granada itself. The last year of Granada's independent history is more a history of secret negotiations than one of Castilian military successes.[44]

The entry of Ferdinand and Isabella into Granada in the first days of 1492 thus had a strongly ceremonial, propagandist character. The terms of the cession made by Boabdil of his crown and kingdom were generous. Boabdil himself was promised a substantial estate nearby, though he soon left to live in Africa. The practice of Islam could continue unimpeded, and the right to operate mosques was confirmed; but the conquerors would pay the expenses of anyone who wished to sell out and go to Africa. Muslim law would continue to operate in Granada, and to all intents the Muslims would continue to exist as an autonomous community under the leadership of their own notables. The Muslims would not be subject to the requirement that they wear a distinctive costume to mark them out from Christians. Jews would not be placed in authority over Granadan Muslims, and indeed the Jews of Granada must either become Christians or leave for Africa in the next few years (this was because the Jews had already been expelled from parts of Christian Andalucia next door a few years earlier). On the other hand, Muslims would not be pressured to convert to Christianity.[45]

---

44 See Miguel Angel Ladero Quesada, *Castilla y la conquista del reino de Granada* (2nd ed., Granada, 1987) for an authoritative discussion of the organisation of the campaign.

45 Harvey, *Islamic Spain,* 314-21.

There was little that was unusual in these provisions. The Granadans were experiencing a transformation in their status from that of Muslim subjects of a Muslim king to *mudéjares*, Muslim subjects of a Christian king; and there were already plenty of *mudéjares* elsewhere in Spain: around 1400 perhaps 20% of the population of the kingdom of Aragon proper were *mudéjares*, while Castile, Navarre and above all Valencia had significant *mudéjar* communities too. It is thus necessary to look at the Spanish Muslim communities beyond Granada and to see how successfully they had survived centuries of Christian rule.[46]

The conquering Christians had adopted a fairly consistent policy. Where Muslims resisted the conquerors to the last, the Christians not merely expelled them but even enslaved some or all of them. Where Muslims surrendered without significant resistance they were guaranteed the continued practice of Islam and considerable autonomy. Those were the two ends of the spectrum, and there were many variations in between. The experience of Minorca provides an eloquent example of Christian attitudes to the subject Muslims. In 1231 the Minorcans accepted Catalan-Aragonese demands that they should become the Muslim vassals of King James I of Aragon and Majorca; the island became an autonomous Muslim enclave subject to the Christian king. In 1287, on the grounds that the Minorcans had acted treasonably, the island was taken by the king of Aragon and

---

46 For the background, see the studies by J. O'Callaghan (Castile and Portugal) and R.I. Burns (Aragon) in James M. Powell (ed.), *Muslims under Latin rule 1100-1300* (Princeton, NJ, 1990)

virtually its entire population was enslaved and deported; they were thus ultimately denied the chance to become *mudéjares*.[47] Key mainland cities such as Córdoba, Seville, Valencia and Murcia were largely repopulated with Christians and Jews from further north, but even there *morerías*, Moorish quarters, often in the suburbs, were allowed to emerge. In most of Spain these communities were formally organised as an *aljama*, a self-governing corporation which was given the authority to collect taxes and to treat with the crown.

One obstacle to the survival of Islam under Christian rule was the opposition of the Muslims themselves. The palliatives offered by the Castilian and Aragonese kings were derided by Muslim religious leaders, who forbade their followers to live under a Christian king.[48] The result in some areas of especially dense *mudéjar* settlement, such as Valencia, was periodic rebellion, which only encouraged the monarchy to adopt a tougher policy towards the Muslims; more generally, there was a drainage of population towards Granada and North Africa. A particular problem was the emigration or on occasion conversion of the old élite families. Headless communities had less means to resist royal encroachment; in the late fifteenth century the Valencian Muslims were under the leadership of successful artisans and there were few well-established, powerful old families. The majority of Muslims in that region were humble peasants. It is,

---

47 E. Lourie, 'Anatomy of Ambivalence,' in E. Lourie, *Crusade and Colonisation. Muslims, Christians and Jews in medieval Aragon* (Aldershot, 1990), section vii, 2-6

48 Harvey, *Islamic Spain,* 56-60.

nonetheless, striking that Muslims continued to live in sizeable numbers as far north as Navarre and Old Castile;[49] in Navarre they were much valued as skilled craftsmen with a speciality in military supplies, while in Castile their brilliant achievements as builders and decorators can still be enjoyed in the Transito Synagogue built at Toledo for Don Samuel Abulafia around 1360 and in the contemporary Alcázar of Seville built for King Pedro the Cruel. The saying went: *Quien non tiene Moros, non tiene oro,* 'whoever does not have Moors does not have gold.' They were the 'Royal Treasure,' the property of the crown or, in some cases, of powerful Christian nobles. It was not so much the poll-tax on Muslims that rulers valued, for this was kept quite low; it was the overall revenues from the soil and from urban taxes on bathhouses, bakeries, butcheries, brothels, casinos and much else that were particularly lucrative. There is no doubt that one reason the kings of Aragon held back from mass expulsions out of Valencia was that the majority of Muslims were agriculturalists, often with special skills, and that the loss of revenue to the crown from a depopulated region was unthinkable.[50] The problem of manpower became even more acute in the fifteenth century, when the continual onslaughts of bubonic plague prevented the population from rising again to early fourteenth-century levels. The *mudéjares* became more, not less, valu-

---

49 Harvey, *Islamic Spain,* 68-97 (Castile), 138-50 (Navarre); M. García Arenal and B. Leroy, *Moros y Judios en Navarra en la Baja Edad Media* (Madrid, 1984)

50 M. Meyerson, *The Muslims of Valencia in the age of Fernando and Isabel* (Berkeley/Los Angeles, 1991).

able to the crown as time passed.

Even so, there is some evidence that the surrender treaties were gradually ignored. By the mid-fourteenth century the large *mudéjar* communities of Valencia and Aragon were under increasing pressure from the Christians. The Muslims found themselves being brought into Christian law courts and Christians were appointed to high office over them, though it has to be said that they probably collected the revenues and left the administration of justice to Muslim deputies.[51] The worsening of the status of the *mudéjares* in Aragon around 1360 can now be seen not as part of a continuous erosion of the rights of the Muslims, but as a steep dip during a period of political crisis when Castile and Aragon were at war and when some Valencian Muslims took advantage of this to forge links with the Castilian enemy; there were also, naturally enough, links to Granada, and it seems that the sultan's name was honoured in Friday prayers in the mosques of Valencia. By the mid-fifteenth century the position of the Muslims had recovered a little, and they could be more confident of securing justice in their own courts, or of avoiding over-taxation; but they had certainly moved some distance from the original surrender terms that their ancestors had received.

The problem the *mudéjares* faced was that, while Jews and Christians were guaranteed special, if limited, rights in Islamic law, going right back to the Koran, Muslims were guaranteed no special rights under Christian canon

---

51 J. Boswell, *The Royal Treasure. Muslim communities under the Crown of Aragon in the fourteenth century* (New Haven, 1977).

law. By the time of Ferdinand II of Aragon the description of them as 'servants of the royal chamber' was current; this implied they were the property of the crown, but it was simply a term adopted from western Christian descriptions of the status of the Jews. Because the rights of the Muslims were not enshrined in canon law, their rights depended on the willingness of the Spanish kings to respect the surrender treaties. It is therefore an interesting paradox that the same Aragonese king, Ferdinand II, who collaborated with his wife Isabella in expelling the Jews, should have permitted the continued practice of Islam beyond the fall of Granada in 1492. 1492 does not mark the end of Spanish Islam; it marks the beginning of a new, if short, period in its history.

The promise to permit the continued practice of Islam in Granada was only gradually compromised. The great Friday Mosque was converted into a cathedral; this was a normal practice of Christian conquerors. The first archbishop, Fray Hernando de Talavera, adopted a cautious approach to conversion, attempting to win the confidence of the Moors by respecting the capitulation agreement; it was too cautious for the royal confidant Francisco Jiménez de Cisneros, archbishop of Toledo, who was scandalised by the guarantees given to the Granadan Muslims, notably by a promise that Christian converts to Islam who were living in Granada before 1492 should not be made to return to Christianity. An obvious worry, too, was that new converts to Christianity were under constant pressure from their old Muslim associates to renounce their new faith. In canon law Cisneros had a number of valid points; Talavera had a greater degree of political awareness, and the result of Cisneros' pressure on the *mudéjares* was a predictable but hopeless revolt against the Catholic Monarchs in 1499- 1500. This provided the new rulers with an excuse to set aside the recent guarantees, and to insist that all Granadan Muslims must become Christians. All remaining mosques were turned into churches, though, interestingly, a few Muslim nobles were apparently allowed to continue to practise Islam privately on their country estates.[52]

Such an anomaly was acceptable since the Granadans alone among Spanish Muslims had been forced to convert. However, by 1502 guarantees were also withdrawn from the Muslims of Castile, whose continued existence in areas that had been purged of Jews ten years earlier must have seemed to Queen Isabella an obvious anomaly. The small kingdom of Navarre, which had abolished the practice of Judaism in 1498, retained its valued Muslim community until 1512, when most of Navarre was acquired by Ferdinand of Aragon. What is astonishing is the lack of application of similar legislation in Aragon and Valencia. A fundamental study of the Valencian Muslims by Mark Meyerson explains why. He distinguishes between the outlook of Isabella (advised by Cisneros), always more fanatical on the question of religious uniformity, and the more pragmatic Ferdinand II, who saw the Muslims, and indeed the Jews, as financial assets in the same way as his predecessors on the Aragonese throne had done. For Isabella, the conversion of

---

52 Harvey, *Isalmic Spain,* 324-37; for further details of the effects of the conquest of Granada, see the works of Miguel Angel Ladero Quesada, *Granada después de la conquista. Repobladores y mudéjares* (2nd ed., Granada, 1988); *Los mudéjares de Castilla y otros estudios de historia medieval andaluza* (Granada, 1989).

a scattering of isolated Muslim communities in Castile was a viable proposition. For Ferdinand, the conversion of perhaps a quarter of his subjects in Aragon proper and in Valencia was not something that could be achieved overnight. Quite apart from the likely problems of mass resistance in areas still entirely inhabited by Muslims, there was the daunting thought that revenue from some of the most profitable assets of the crown might suffer badly; this was a time when the monarchy needed to foster economic recovery in the Aragonese realms after a period of civil war and uneven economic performance. The result was that Islam was quite simply allowed to survive for another generation.[53] It is now thought unlikely that Ferdinand was unduly disturbed by the danger that the Turks would use the *mudéjares* as a Fifth Column, since the furthest the Turks had reached so far was Otranto in southern Italy, a long way eastward. In 1525 political trouble, compounded by the renewed fear that Muslims were interfering with new conversions, prompted Charles V (Carlos I of Spain) to order the mass baptism of the *mudéjares* of Valencia and Aragon. Even then the practice of Islam continued in secret until the early seventeenth century, when renewed rebellion resulted in a mass expulsion of the people who were now known as the Moriscos; by this time fear of the Turks had emerged as an issue.[54] Cut off from the rest of the Islamic world, writing more and more in a Spanish

---

53 Meyerson, *Muslims of Valencia*, passim.

54 S. Haliczer, *Inquisition and society in the Kingdom of Valencia, 1478-1834* (Berkeley/Los Angeles, 1990); W. Monter, *Frontiers of heresy. The Spanish Inquisition from the Basque lands to Sicily* (Cambridge, 1990).

vernacular now called *aljamiado* or *aljamía*, the Moriscos developed a subterranean culture based on the compromise between public observance of Christianity and the private observance of a watered down form of Islam in which even knowledge of Arabic evaporated.[55] It will be seen that the experience of the Jews in Spain was strikingly similar.

The events in Granada of January 1492 were not part of an immediate programme for making all Spaniards Christian. In a sense, of course, they had resulted in something connected but different: all Spaniards were now under Christian rule. The next ten years proved that it was not an enormous step to making all Castilian subjects Christian; Aragon, as ever, preserved its complex and separate identity.

III. The Expulsion of the Jews

The status of the Jews in Spain was only superficially similar to that of the Muslims. Whereas the Muslims possessed a state of their own in Spain until 1492, and many states outside Spain, the Jews had no option but to live under the rule of Christians (or, in Granada, Muslims). Whereas the Muslims included a substantial rural population, the Jews were predominantly townspeople, and may have been more evenly spread across the Ibe-

---

55 A. Chejne, *Islam and the West: the Moriscos. A cultural and social history* (Albany, NY, 1983); L. Cardaillac, *Moriscos et Chrétiens. Un affrontement polémique (1492-1640)* (Paris, 1977); A. Domínguez Ortiz and B. Vincent, *Historia de los Moriscos* (Madrid, 1978).

rian kingdoms; numerically they were hardly significant, with perhaps 2% of the population by 1400. Whereas the Moorish aristocracy had largely disappeared through emigration or assimilation, there remained powerful and ancient Jewish families that constituted an intellectual, political and economic élite.[56] Whereas Muslim advisers were insignificant at court by the fifteenth century, the Jews had a lengthy history of serving the crown as financial agents. Finally, whereas the Muslims remained strikingly loyal to Islam until the mass conversions of 1499 onwards, those of Jewish descent were by the fifteenth century divided into two groups: people openly of the Jewish religion; and converts to Christianity, who themselves subdivided into other groups, those who were committed Christians and those who accepted baptism as a camouflage for continuing observance of Judaism, or in some cases for religious scepticism. These differences helped dictate the contrasting experience of Jews and Muslims in 1492.

Like the Muslims, the Jews were seen by the Spanish kings as a valuable asset; in Catalonia they might be taxed more heavily than Christians; in Majorca King James III praised them 'because they live mainly by trade.' While by 1400 in most areas of Europe the Jews were forced into unpopular and dubious occupations such as moneylending, which was technically forbidden by Christian, and indeed Jewish and Islamic, law, in Spain a wider variety of occupations, including international trade, the jewellery industry and specialised agriculture

---

56 L. Suarez Fernández, *Les juifs espagnols au Moyen Age* (Paris, 1983), 113

(such as wine-making), can be identified. There had been periods of cultural efflorescence, in eleventh-century Granada, then often called 'Granada of the Jews,' in thirteenth-century Girona and Toledo, when scientific study and translation work were combined with the mysticism of the *Kabbalah*. Such successes depended in high degree on royal favour; some historians have talked optimistically of the easy coexistence (*convivencia*) of all three religions at this time. What changed in the late Middle Ages was the result of an intensification of preaching campaigns against the Jews, and the spread of popular anti-Jewish feeling which was greatly accentuated by the economic crisis that followed the Black Death, and by competition between an emergent Christian urban middle class and Jewish office-holders, shopkeepers and artisans. The Jews acquired their traditional role as scapegoats for failures with which they had nothing to do: during the Black Death itself, there were accusations that Jews were poisoning the wells in Toledo and elsewhere, even though Jews too died in massive numbers from the plague; the result was that to mortality from plague was added mortality from pogroms.

Particular enemies of the Jews were the Dominican and Franciscan friars, who led missions to the Jews, and who also fanned the flames of hatred. In 1391 friars preaching against the Jews in Andalucia unleashed a series of pogroms that spread northwards to Castile proper, to Valencia and Barcelona, to Majorca and even, by 1392, to the overseas Aragonese possession of Sicily.[57] The

57 P. Wolff, 'The 1391 pogrom in Spain. Social crisis or not?', *Past and Present*, no. 50 (1971), 4-18; M. Mollat and P. Wolff, *The Popular revolutions of the late Middle Ages* (London, 1973), 211-25.

result was a sizeable increase in forced or panic conversions to Christianity, above all in the Aragonese lands where cities such as Barcelona saw the Jewish community collapse in ruins. In Majorca, riots against the Jews originated in a rural protest against the policies of the Governor-General of the island in a period of agrarian recession; unable to reach the hated governor, the mob broke into the Jewish quarter, or *Call*, of the capital city and sacked it. In 1435 further rumours resulted in the Jews of Majorca being given the choice of conversion or death. There was a mass baptism in the church of Santa Eulalia, on the edge of the Call. Majorcan Judaism had come to an abrupt end.[58]

Yet people did not simply forget who was of Jewish origin. The Majorcan converts acquired the pejorative name of *Xuetas*, which probably means 'little Jews.' Until the twentieth century they were subject to social discrimination in Majorca, even though all Jewish practices had long ceased.[59] The problem in fifteenth-century Spain, Majorca apart, was the existence side by side of Jews and ex-Jews, who in any case still counted in Jewish law as Jews, and who were blood relatives, often

---

58 A. Lionel Isaacs, *The Jews of Majorca* (London, 1936); K. Moore, *Those of the Street. The Catholic-Jews of Mallorca. A study in urban cultural change* (Notre Dame, IN, 1976).

59 Moore, *Those of the Street*, passim; B. Porcel, *Los Chuetas mallorquines. Quince siglos de racismo* (6th ed., Palma de Mallorca, 1986); Angela S. Selke, *The conversos of Majorca. Life and death in a crypto-Jewish community in seventeenth-century Spain* (Jerusalem, 1988).

neighbours, of Jews.[60] The *conversos*, or New Christians, were remarkably successful outside Majorca in rising to the top ranks of the civil administration, the universities and even the church: the most famous example is perhaps Paul of Burgos (Pablo de Santa Maria) who started as a rabbi in the mid-fourteenth century, became a priest, and rose to be bishop of Burgos. Around 1500, the entourage of Cisneros contained a number of converted Jews who, as priests and professors, helped in the compilation of his multi-lingual Complutensian Bible, the intention of which was not to honour the Jews, by printing the Hebrew text of the Bible, so much as to make plain that the Christians alone understood the true meaning of the Old Testament.

The success of the *conversos* was resented by the established nobility, who still found it convenient to marry their children to wealthy *converso* families, and even more by newly successful Old Christians in the towns, who competed with *conversos* for royal favour and for the position of city governor. The success of the *conversos* is truly impressive, comparable, perhaps, to that of the emancipated Jews of nineteenth-century Europe. On the other hand, committed Jews did not entirely disappear from royal favour: despite constant attempts in Castile and Aragon, the church and the parliamentary assemblies failed to ensure that Jews would be prevented

---

60 A. Mackay, 'The Hispanic-*Converso* predicament,' *Transactions of the Royal Historical Society,* ser. 5, xxxv (1985), 159-79; J.H. Edwards, 'Religious belief and social conformity: the *converso* problem in late medieval Córdoba,' *Transactions of the Royal Historical Society,* ser. 5, xxxi (1981).

from holding office over Christians. King Pedro the Cruel, who was rather old-fashioned in his relations with Jews and Muslims, appointed Don Samuel Abulafia as his *Tesorero Mayor*, or Treasurer, and royal finances recovered as a result of Abulafia's imaginative policies.[61] Pedro's rival Henry of Trastámara denounced his half-brother for his favours to the Jews, but on becoming king he acted little differently. As late as the campaign to conquer Granada, a certain Samuel Abulafia was in charge of supplies for the Christian troops, and his Jewish colleagues at court included Rabbi Abraham Seneor and the eminent scholar Don Isaac Abravanel.[62]

Although largely a phenomenon of the sixteenth century, there are signs as early as the mid-fifteenth of attempts to discriminate against those with Jewish blood, irrespective of their commitment to Christianity. An uprising in Toledo in 1449 culminated in demands that the city government should exclude all *conversos* from holding office; under the statute that was passed, *conversos* were even prevented from giving evidence against Old Christians in court.[63] Jewish ancestry became a taint that could not be removed by baptism. Even within the Church there were occasional attempts to persecute those of Jewish descent, such as the bishops of Segovia and of Calahorra, the former of whom was in fact a noted enemy of

---

61 L. Díaz Martin, *Los oficiales de Pedro I de Castilla* (Madrid, 1975), 100-2.

62 H. Kamen, *Inquisition and society in sixteenth-century Spain* (London, 1985), 9, amending 'David' to Samuel.

63 Kamen, *Inquisition,* 25; Kamen, *Spain,* 39.

the Jews. The problem was that a significant proportion of converts continued to practise Judaism in secret; Old Christian critics argued that the conversion had often been superficial and that the rush of Jews to the font in fifteenth-century Spain had created a new danger: heretical Christians whose heresy consisted in the continuing observance of Judaism or, in the case of Muslim converts, Islam.

The question of the sincerity of the converts, which in any case can only be answered case by case, then and now aroused much controversy.[64] In the late Middle Ages rabbis of Spanish origin, such as Shimeon ben Zemah Duran, a Majorcan exile domiciled in Algiers, debated whether the *conversos* were still Jews; this was largely a question of Jewish law, affecting their status as witnesses in court, their marriages, and so on; but it was also no secret that throughout Spain Jewish practices remained alive in New Christian communities.[65] Was this a matter of religious belief or of tradition and culture? *Conversos* continued to prepare food in Jewish style, avoiding pork and cooking with olive oil rather than lard; sometimes, too, they purchased meat from animals slaughtered according to Jewish law. Judaism, it is often remarked, is not just a religion but a way of life, in which almost every action is conducted according to the

---

64 B. Netanyahu, *Don Isaac Abravanel. Statesman and philosopher* (2nd ed., Philadelphia, 1968); B. Netanyahu, *The Marranos of Spain, from the late fourteenth to the early sixteenth century according to contemporary Hebrew sources* (2nd ed., New York, 1973).

65 I. Epstein, *The responsa of Rabbi Simon ben Zemah Duran, as a source of the history of the Jews in north Africa* (London, 1930).

rules of an elaborate religious culture. The transition to
the religious culture of Christianity was a difficult one in
the fifteenth century. Instinctive reactions, such as crossing oneself on passing a church, were lacking in the
converso; they could be construed, by fierce critics, as
signs of lack of commitment.[66] Perhaps, too, the extent
to which *conversos* tried to achieve an intellectual compromise between their old and their new religion should
not be underestimated. There was a long tradition in
Spain of sharing in the wedding processions of other
religions; Muslims even attended the Corpus Christi cele-
brations in fifteenth-century Valencia.[67] It may not have
appeared anomalous to an elderly convert from Judaism
to leave money for the lighting of the synagogue in her
will, and yet to be buried in a Christian cemetery. Nor
was it unusual for converts to continue to live in the
same houses or streets as unconverted relatives and
friends.[68]

The Church under Cisneros, enthusiastically supported
by the Crown, sought to bring this problem under control in the 1480's. The Inquisition, which had existed in
a fairly dormant state in Aragon since the thirteenth century, was re-established as the first Spanish-wide institution, active in Castile and Aragon primarily against re-

---

66 For an appreciation of this dilemma, see the articles by Mackay
and Edwards cited above.

67 Meyerson, *Muslims of Valencia*, 227

68 Joseph ha-Cohen and the Anonymous Corrector, *The Vale of
Tears (Emek Habacha)*, transl. Harry S. May (The Hague, 1971),
65.

lapsed converts.[69] Its power against unconverted Jews was far more restricted, and applied mainly to cases where Jews interfered in its work, for instance by attempting to draw *conversos* back to Judaism. Rapidly the Inquisition identified leading *conversos* who had acquired public office and who were said to practise Judaism in secret; in the most serious cases they were burnt at the stake. The first public execution, in February 1481, followed rumours of an uprising and was aimed at prominent public figures in Seville such as the city official and lawyer Juan Fernández Abulafia.[70] More radical means were also used to separate Jews from converts. Converts could be required to live outside the Jewish quarter that existed in many cities. More drastically, the Jews could be expelled from individual cities, as happened in Seville in 1483. These local expulsions were a guide to future intentions throughout Spain.

For some very committed *conversos*, the presence of large Jewish communities was an offence that could only be removed by their wholesale removal from Spain. The view that New Christians anxious to convince the Church of their commitment to their new religion encouraged the plans for a mass expulsion has been presented by Professor Netanyahu in controversial studies of the events of 1492, in which he underplays the existence of large numbers of very uncommitted *conversos* alongside the

---

69 Kamen, *Inquisition*, 31-43.

70 Kamen, *Inquisition*, 31-2.

zealots.[71] Yet his view carries a certain amount of weight. The enemies of the Jews in 1492 included leading churchmen of Jewish descent, including, apparently, the inquisitor Torquemada. Important too is Netanyahu's insight that the Catholic Monarchs saw the decree of expulsion as a means to secure a further wave of conversions. They very probably expected most Jews to remain in Spain, as Christian converts. Although there was a danger that these converts would be half-hearted, they would all fall under the control of the Inquisition; they would no longer be subject to the influence of Jewish kin or neighbours, and they would no longer have access to synagogues, kosher butchers and other Jewish institutions. Judaism might, of course, go underground, and the Inquisition may have exaggerated its ability, even using the most ruthless means, to prevent this happening, as it did. Yet initially the idea of securing a mass conversion seemed to be working. Abraham Seneor, a leading financier, close to the Crown, who functioned as head of the Jewish communities of Castile, accepted baptism to escape expulsion, and took the new name of Coronel.[72] Later, though, the Coronel family appears prominently among the crypto-Jews of Spain and Portugal. Another figure of equal standing, Isaac Abravanel or

---

71 Netanyahu, *Marranos,* goes so far as to insist that the Marranos were not Jews; cf. the views of the eminent specialist H. Beinart, *Conversos on trial. The Inquisition in Ciudad Real* (Jerusalem, 1981), 242. Kamen, *Inquisition,* 27-8, offers a judicious appraisal of a debate much influenced by modern events; see also J. Israel, *European Jewry in the age of Mercantilism 1550-1750* (2nd ed., Oxford, 1989), 3.

72 Kamen, *Inquisition,* 15, points out that by converting Seneor remained a member of the royal court.

Abarbanel, offers a striking contrast; this cosmopolitan figure, knowledgeable in philosophy, refused to convert and brought his great talent to the court of Naples. It is likely that both these figures promised Ferdinand and Isabella a large sum of money if they would revoke the order of expulsion. This was not, as often described, a last minute bribe; it was a standard way in which medieval monarchs had raised money from the Jews. It was hard for the Spanish Jews to believe that the threat of expulsion was not yet another excuse to raise some money. Ferdinand, true to character, is said to have seen the advantages of accepting the offer, but Isabella was fortified in her resolve by the tempestuous Torquemada; in the end, Ferdinand too was keen to claim the initiative.[73]

The orders were applied in the first instance to Aragon and Castile, but they were rapidly extended to Aragon's possessions of Sardinia and Sicily.[74] Estimates of the number who left Spain vary, and a figure of 100,000 may be too high; assessments of the effect of their loss on the Spanish economy also vary, though many historians have insisted that the loss of the financial and productive skills of the Spanish Jews was a serious blow to Spain on the eve of its rise to world power.[75] (On the other hand, many *conversos* continued in the same occupation, and also gained access to new occupations for-

73 Kamen, *Inquisition*, 14-15.

74 C. Roth, *History of the Jews in Italy*, (Philadelphia, 1946), 252-68.

75 F. Braudel, *The Mediterranean and the Mediterranean world at the time of Philip II*, 2 vols (London, 1972-3), ii.802-26.

bidden to Jews; another point is that Italian and Flemish settlers in Spain were offering similar skills to the expelled Jews).[76] What is certain is that those who left Spain experienced terrible misery. Many were sold into slavery or even drowned by ruthless shipowners in the Mediterranean.[77] Few western states would welcome them; there was the spectacle, not to be repeated till the 1940's, of Jews confined to rotting hulks outside ports where they could not land.

But opportunities for refuge did exist. Within Iberia, many took the land route to Portugal and Navarre. The Portuguese king was less than certain that he wanted the great mass of refugees on his hands. In 1496-7, under strong diplomatic pressure from Spain, he decreed the expulsion of all unconverted Jews, whether native or exiles from Spain; on second thought, perhaps fearful of the economic effects, he forced the majority to be baptised; some were pulled to the font by their hair. The result was the creation of an even larger pool of crypto-Jews in Portugal than in Spain, some of whom have persisted to the twentieth century.[78] Navarre seemed more welcoming at first, but Castilian influence was growing in this little kingdom, not least by way of interference by the Inquisition; in 1498 the Navarrese Jews were given the choice of exile or conversion. Since there was no

---

76 J. Israel, *European Jewry in the age of Mercantilism 1550--1750* (2nd ed., Oxford, 1989), 27

77 Joseph ha-Cohen, *Vale of Tears*, 65-66.

78 C. Roth, *A History of the Marranos* (Philadelphia, 1932), 54-60.

way out of Navarre except into Castile, Aragon or France, from all of which Jews were banned at risk of their life, Navarre's Jews virtually all converted to Christianity, including those who had escaped from Castile precisely in order not to convert.[79] With the fall of Navarre's Jewries, Judaism came to an end, officially at least, in the Iberian peninsula.

Others escaped entirely from Iberia. There was a large immigration into Morocco, where large Jewish communities already existed under Muslim rule. The papacy allowed Jews to settle in Rome, but under increasingly restrictive conditions; in northern Italy Ferrara was one of the few cities to extend a warm welcome. The Aragonese king of Naples, Ferrante I, sought to take advantage of the mistakes of his ally Ferdinand II of Aragon; he permitted Spanish and Sicilian Jews to settle, and was especially glad to attract the skills of Isaac Abravanel and his sons. As a ruler who was keen to stimulate small scale industry, Ferrante had good hopes of benefiting from the arrival of thousands of Jewish artisans.[80] However, the Jews soon became enmeshed in the chaos of the French invasion of Italy (1494); the eventual triumph of Ferdinand of Aragon as king of Naples, by 1506, left the Jews in a dangerous position, though it was not until 1511 that a decree was issued

---

79 B. Gampel, *The last Jews on Iberian soil. Navarrese Jewry 1497/8* (Berkeley/Los Angeles, 1989).

80 David Abulafia, 'The Crown and the economy under Ferrante I of Naples (1458-1494)', in T. Dean, C. Wickham, eds, *City and Countryside in late medieval and Renaissance Italy, Essays presented to Philip Jones* (London, 1990), 137.

expelling the Jews and the so-called *neofiti*, descendants of south Italian Jews whose commitment to Christianity was considered doubtful. Even so, a few wealthy and illustrious Jews were allowed to remain, on the grounds of their usefulness, and the expulsion was notable for its many exceptions. Not for the first time, we see Ferdinand adopting a more pragmatic approach than Isabella, now dead, would ever have done. A final expulsion took place fifty years later under Charles V, the same ruler who, paradoxically, extended his protection to the Jews of Germany about the same time.[81]

Nothing, however, compared to the welcome offered to the Jews by the Ottoman sultan, whose reasoning was not so very different from that of Ferrante, and who did not question the fact of being ruler over many religions. Salonika became an especially important centre of Jewish settlement; the origins of its Jewish inhabitants were commemorated in the existence of different synagogues for the Aragonese, Catalan, Andalucian, Castilian and Sicilian Jews.[82] Last but by no means least, a few leaders, strongly influenced by the mysticism of the Spanish *Kabbalah*, headed for the Ottoman controlled Holy Land and established settlements in Galilee.[83] The events of

---

81 Roth, *Jews of Italy*, 278-88; Israel, *European Jewry*, 15-16; he also brought the Inquisition to Portugal.

82 R. Patal, *The vansihed worlds of Jewry* (London, 1981), 88-93; Israel, *European Jewry*, 32, 196.

83 See the studies by A. David in A. Carmel, P. Schaefer, Y. Ben-Artzi (eds), *The Jewish settlement in Palestine 634-1881* (Wiesbaden, 1990), especially 80-1.

1492 had stimulated the belief that Redemption was nigh and that the Messiah was about to come. But even there lively disputes arose between leaders such as the Spanish exile Jacob Berab and other rabbis who had lived for a time as forced converts in Spain over the status of the Marranos.

For the expulsion was a tremendous shock.[84] There had been Jews in Spain since the days of the Emperor Hadrian; they had played a full part in the rediscovery of classical philosophical and scientific texts in twelfth and thirteenth-century Spain; they had occupied positions very close to the Spanish kings. To the modern historian, the erosion of the Aragonese communities after 1391 and the constant stream of converts in the fifteenth century seem clear signs that Spanish Jewry was being boxed into a corner. Besides, expulsions had been going ahead for two hundred years; a novelty when they began in England and parts of northern France around 1290, they had been repeated again and again thereafter. Indeed, the years around 1492 saw expulsions all over Europe: from Ravenna in 1491, from Florence in 1494, and from many German cities, often after violent attacks on the Jews.[85] The Spanish Jews were aware of a crisis on the eve of 1492, but they believed they had the means to prevent it. The parallel with the Jews in central Europe in the early

---

84 Israel, *European Jewry*, 31, talks of the Expulsion as 'the greatest single disaster to descend on the Jews between the destruction of the Second Temple and Hitler's holocaust.'

85 Israel, *European Jewry*, 7-8.

to mid-twentieth century is uncomfortably close.

One measure of the shock is the way the Jews of Spanish descent, known as the 'Sephardim' (literally, 'Spaniards') retained a culture that was dominated by Spain. Their everyday language was the Castilian Spanish of the fifteenth century, known as Ladino or Judeo-Spanish, written, however, in Hebrew characters. Spanish cuisine survived as far east as Turkey. Distinctive rituals and liturgies, full of poems (*piyyutim*) by Medieval Spanish Jewish authors were carried eastwards. Most striking of all is the survival of beautiful secular songs in Ladino, whose music and words often hark back to medieval Spain.[86] Associated with this was the sense among Sephardic Jews of their descent from Spanish *hidalgos*, who had carried swords and ridden steeds, and, ultimately from the nobility of biblical Jerusalem. Leading families such as Abravanel and Abulafia insisted they were descended from King David.[87] Asserting their right to leadership, the Sephardim imposed their culture and even the Spanish language on less resilient communities of native Balkan and Turkish Jews.[88]

---

86 These songs are still regularly broadcast on Israel Radio, as is the news in Ladino; good modern recordings have been made in the U.S.A. under the unfortunate label *Voice of the Turtle*. For the culture of the exiles see R. Barnett and W. Schwab (eds), *The Sephardi Heritage*, vol. 2, *The western Sephardim* (Gibraltar, 1990).

87 H.J. Zimmels, *Ashkenazim and Sephardim. Their relations, differences, and problems as reflected in the rabbinical responsa* (London, 1958), 279-87.

88 Patai, *Vanished worlds*, 90-1.

For the *conversos* too the expulsion was a shock. They found themselves in a state of suspension, exiled not from Spain but to the margins of Spanish society, not always regarded as Christians but often distinctive by customs, outlook and name. In 1498 Samuel Abulafia of Toledo was arrested, brought before the Inquisition and then, to his obvious relief, acquitted of all charges; but he decided that his origins were too obvious and changed his name to Diego Gómez.[89] In the sixteenth century increasing insistence on pure Christian ancestry (*limpieza de sangre*) meant that even such subterfuges did not always succeed when a *converso* was seeking the hand of a noble heiress or was hoping to gain high office. The result was that *conversos* tended to marry *conversas*, making it easier for Jewish practices to be handed down in secret. The most committed crypto-Jews, dismissively known as *Marranos* (literally, 'pigs') managed to observe a number of Jewish feast days and might even succeed in avoiding pork, in lighting the Sabbath candles, in burying their dead secretly; but knowledge of the Hebrew language and liturgy rapidly declined, and the need to avoid detection resulted in the postponement of important events such as the Day of Atonement and the abandonment of circumcision of newly-born sons. Aware of Jewish subterfuges, inquisitors would warn against those who had a pot of pork stew bubbling away at the front door: a clear attempt to blow away all whiff of suspicion! At home, mothers did most to transmit some knowledge of Judaism to their children; in the street,

---

89 J. Gómez-Mener Fuentes, 'Un judío converso de 1498. Diego Gómez de Toledo (Semuel Abolafia) y su proceso,' *Sefarad,* xxxiii (1973), 45-110.

still more in church, their Christian conduct had to be exemplary. Where there was common ground between Judaism and Christianity, the Marranos felt safer; they made extensive use of the psalms in their prayers, even if that meant using the official Catholic translation into Latin, the Vulgate. The Christian practice of kneeling in prayer was adopted.[90] In fact, Marrano religion was in significant degree a mishmash of Jewish and Christian practices, at the core of which lay, nonetheless, an exclusive personal commitment to the Jewish religion. The emotional commitment was all the greater since the Marranos were acutely conscious of the suspicion under which they were held by Old Christians.

For a time it seemed that the Inquisition had won its battle against the Marranos. By the middle of the sixteenth century Majorca and Portugal were perhaps the only areas in which resistance persisted on a large scale; but towards the end of the century Portuguese Marranos settling in Spain, where they actually felt safer, reintroduced vigorous crypto-Judaism to Castile. Conversion to Christianity did not, after all, result in the integration of the Iberian Jews into the dominant society; in many ways the *conversos* filled the gap left by the disappearance of confessed Jews, even to the extent of taking on the mantle of a persecuted minority. But they also compensated for their despised status by taking secret pride in all those things for which they stood condemned: their Jewish blood; their preference for Judaism over Christianity. The attempt to coerce them into being good Christians backfired, not least because discrimination was based on

90 Roth, *Marranos*, 175-8.

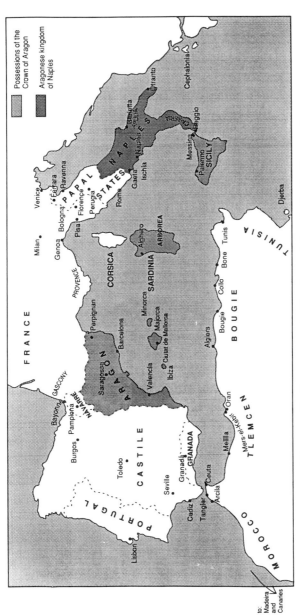

The Western Mediterranean in the Age of the Catholic Monarchs

Possessions of the Crown of Aragon

Aragonese kingdom of Naples

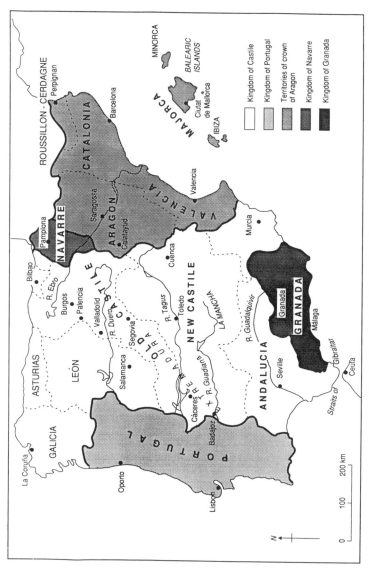

Spain Under the Catholic Monarchs

ROUSSILLON - CERDAGNE
Perpignan
CATALONIA
Barcelona

MINORCA
BALEARIC
ISLANDS
MAJORCA
Ciutat
de Mallorca
IBIZA

NAVARRE
Pamplona
ARAGON
Saragossa
Calatayud
VALENCIA
Valencia

ASTURIAS
La Coruña
GALICIA
Oporto

LEÓN
Bilbao
R. Ebro
Burgos
Palencia
Valladolid
R. Duero
Segovia
Salamanca
OLD CASTILE

Cáceres
R. Guadiana
Badajoz

PORTUGAL
Lisboa

Cuenca
NEW CASTILE
R. Tagus
Toledo
LA MANCHA

Murcia

R. Guadalquivir
ANDALUCIA
Seville
GRANADA
Granada
Málaga
Gibraltar
Ceuta
Straits of

Kingdom of Castile
Kingdom of Portugal
Territories of crown of Aragon
Kingdom of Navarre
Kingdom of Granada

N

0   100   200 km

their lineage as well as on the suspicion of heresy.

IV. The exploration of the Atlantic

It may appear ironic that the Christianisation of Spain was proceeding just as Castile seized the lead in the conquest of further non-Christian territories. The Spanish monarchs continued to harbour long-standing ambitions in the Maghrib (north-west Africa), where both Castilian and Aragonese rulers had conducted wars in the past. The prospect of ruling a vast non-Christian population was eagerly anticipated by Ferdinand II. Moreover, the late fifteenth century saw the acquisition and settlement by Castile of the Canary Islands, whose indigenous population was neither Christian nor Muslim. The contact of the Castilians with the prehistoric cultures of the Canaries influenced later attitudes to the peoples of central and south America who were about to have their existence revealed. Thus the continuities from the late Middle Ages must not be underestimated. The discovery of unsuspected continents was a shock to the geographers, but the problem how to deal with peoples who had never had the chance to hear the word of Christ had been receiving attention for several decades.[91]

Exploration of Atlantic waters took off after the opening of the direct sea-route from Italy and Majorca to Flanders and England, around 1277. Even before then it seems that Genoese and possibly Catalan ships were being de-

---

91 J. Muldoon, *Popes, lawyers and infidels. The Church and the non-Christian world 1250-1500* (Liverpool, 1979).

flected southwards from the Straits of Gibraltar and were visiting the ports of Atlantic Morocco. Ancient geographers already knew of the Canaries, but it was probably the Genoese who made the first systematic exploration of them in the early fourteenth century; one island, Lanzarote, supposedly bears the name of the Genoese mariner Lanzelotto Malocello. The islands began to appear on the excellent portolan charts prepared in Majorca and Italy in the fourteenth century, and were described by the humanist Petrarch; there are even signs that ships swinging further out into the Atlantic happened upon the uninhabited Madeira archipelago and on the equally empty Azores.[92] It is difficult to disentangle long-held beliefs about mysterious islands to the west from exact geographical knowledge; in any case, fact and fancy converged as the Atlantic islands were revealed.

The first to stake a major claim to the Canaries was James III, king of Majorca, a nominal vassal of the king of Aragon. In around 1340, on the eve of the re-absorption of his kingdom into Aragon, James licensed several expeditions to the Canaries; the assumption was that control of islands off the west coast of Africa, if combined with control of the Balearic islands off the north coast of Africa, would permit the launching of an ambitious crusade into the Maghrib, and would grant access to the plentiful gold supplies of the rivers south of the Sahara desert. Gold that would otherwise be drawn into the Islamic economy could be diverted to Christian uses.

---

92 Felipe Fernández-Armesto, *Before Columbus. Exploration and colonisation from the Mediterranean to the Atlantic, 1229-1492* (London, 1987), 151-68.

The Majorcans sent missionaries to the Canaries, and there were limited attempts at settlement.[93] A few years later, an exiled Castilian prince, Luis de la Cerda, secured the agreement of Pope Clement VI for a similar scheme, involving lordship over the Canaries and over the small island of Jalita near Tunisia. Such grand dreams could also serve as a cover for more basic ambitions; Genoese, Castilian, Portuguese, even Norman French mariners began to contest the Canaries, notably the Frenchmen Jean de Béthencourt and Gadifer de la Salle just after 1400.[94] The Catalans, having done so much to open up the route to the Canaries, then retired to the armchair occupation of cartographers and left the actual exploration and exploitation to others.

The major new force that replaced them, and that made extensive use of their cartographic knowledge, was Portugal. Long-distance Portuguese trade had long been dominated by resident Genoese businessmen in Lisbon; but in the early fifteenth century, under the impetus of Prince Henry 'the Navigator', the Portuguese began to take a decisive initiative. Contrary to popular belief, Henry was in many ways an old-fashioned figure, more interested in the crusade against the African Moors than in precise science, the heir, in fact, of the ideals of the early Majorcan claimants to the Canaries and to Luis de la

---

93 Fernández-Armesto, *Before Columbus,* 156-9, 171; F. Sevillano Colom, 'Los viajes medievales desde Mallorca a Canarias,' *Anuario de estudios atlánticos,* xxiii (1978), 27-57.

94 Fernández-Armesto, *Before Columbus,* 185-84.

Cerda.[95] He had an eye too on the gold of Black Africa, particularly since gold shortages were beginning to constrict the European economy, though of course his main concern was the diversion of gold away from Muslim treasuries where it could be used to strengthen Islam against western assaults. His career began in 1415 with his participation in the Portuguese conquest of the important trading centre of Ceuta, on the African shore directly opposite Gibraltar; Portugal demonstrated that it was already prepared to carry the *reconquista* into Africa, an ambition its rulers shared with the kings of Castile and Aragon. Also in Atlantic waters, Portuguese captains from Henry's entourage rediscovered and laid claim to Porto Santo and its neighbour Madeira around 1420, and the islands began to be colonised; during the fifteenth century they became centres of sugar production, making it possible for western merchants, notably the Flemings, to obtain sugar well away from the Muslim world which was a major traditional source of supply.[96] Sugar ensured the survival of what were at first precarious colonies of quarrelsome adventurers, desperadoes and ex-convicts; much sugar was despatched to Flanders, and fine paintings obtained in return can still be seen in the impressive Cathedral Museum of Funchal, the capital of Madeira. Flemish interests were even more prominent in

---

95 P.E. Russell, *Prince Henry the Navigator* (London, 1960); P.E. Russell, *Prince Henry the Navigator: the rise and fall of a culture hero* (Oxford, 1984).

96 R. Carita, *História da Madeira (1420-1566). Povoamento e Produção açucareira* (Funchal, 1989); L. de Albuquerque, *Introdução ô história dos descobrimentos portugueses* (4th ed., Lisbon, 1989), 159-63.

the exploitation of the distant Azores, for there the colonists included many Flemings, who developed the pastoral and agrarian economy and helped build a busy grain trade towards Flanders.[97] Thus these islands were not simply eccentric conquests; they were rapidly integrated into the European economy, with the help of Portuguese, Genoese and north European merchants and shippers. In addition, the foundation of trading stations on the coasts of Africa and the settlement of the hot, unproductive Cape Verde Islands secured Portugal's mastery in Atlantic waters.[98]

Castile appeared to take a backseat role. Like Portugal, Castile was heavily involved with Genoese traders. The Genoese colony in Seville serviced the needs of Italian merchants bound from the Mediterranean to the Atlantic; Genoese credit was of longstanding importance to royal finances; the Castilian fleet had been created by Genoese admirals during the Hundred Years' War. The active merchant communities of Cantabria and the Basque ports were mainly involved in trade to western France, England and Flanders, and also to Seville, where they linked up with the Genoese and from where they sometimes penetrated into the Mediterranean. The Basque sailors may have known a fair amount about Atlantic waters, but they took no obvious lead in Castilian exploration of the Atlantic. Only in the 1470's did Castile begin

---

97 C. Verlinden, *The beginnings of modern colonization* (Ithaca, NY, 1970), 181-95; A. Vieira, *O Comércio inter-insular nos séculos XV e XVI. Madeira, Açores e Canàrias* (Funchal, 1987).

98 Verlinden, *Beginnings,* 161-80.

to make determined efforts to press its own claims in the
Canaries and west Africa; conflict with Portugal, which
was still smarting from Isabella's decision to marry an
Aragonese prince, stimulated the Catholic Monarchs to
carry the struggle beyond Iberia into Portugal's early
African colonies. In 1479 plans were announced for a
gold mining colony on the Guinea coast, right under the
noses of the Portuguese. The Catholic Monarchs also
began to press their rights in the Canaries, after they
purchased rights over Tenerife, Palma and Grand Canary
from an existing Castilian noble claimant. Here too they
tried to trample on Portuguese rights, and an expedition
was sent out from Castile to the Canaries in 1478; its
leaders were granted considerable authority, and it was
not yet clear that the Catholic Monarchs planned to take
much interest in the internal affairs of these distant islands. What secured the Canaries for Castile was not so
much this expedition as the Castilian-Portuguese peace
treaty of 1479, signed at Alcaçovas. Portuguese claims
in Morocco, on the Guinea coast, in Madeira, the Azores
and the Cape Verde Islands were all accepted by the
Castilians, but Castilian overlordship in the Canaries was
recognised by Portugal. Even so, this was as much a
statement of theory as of fact; the largest Canary islands
still had to be subdued, and very many of the western
settlers were from Portugal or Genoa. There were endless complaints against the leaders of the Castilian expeditions during the 1480's, and as a result the monarchy
began to take a more direct interest in Canarian affairs,
and the two monarchs added the Canaries to their already long list of royal titles. Alfonso Fernández de Lugo
was appointed hereditary *adelantado* of the islands, with
the task of organising the settlement of the islands and

the exploitation of native labour; perhaps the very fact they were so far away made the Catholic Monarchs aware of the need for relatively tight control.[99]

The acquisition of the islands brought little benefit to the Castilians back home. Economic conditions were harsh; the hot, dry climate left the islands unproductive, and the inhabitants depended heavily on imports from Castile, offering in return a few dyestuffs and pastoral products.[100] The native population of Guanches and other peoples resisted conquest, and the debate about their rights was well established before Castile acquired sovereignty over the islands. In 1436 King Duarte of Portugal informed the pope that Portuguese interests in the Canaries were determined by the wish to convert the inhabitants; his letter describes with wonder the conditions of life in a prehistoric society where writing, a common faith and money are unknown; they are 'nearly wild men . . . lacking normal social intercourse, living in the country like animals.' Equally, the king was worried that independent adventurers were attacking the Guanches and making impossible the slow but steady process of winning them to the Church. A later pope, writing nearly forty years later, praised the Franciscan missionary Fray Alonso de Bolaños for his work in converting the native inhabitants of Tenerife: 'those who hitherto have not known God, now wish to take up the Catholic

---

99 J.F. Ramsey, *Spain: the rise of the first world power* (Alabama, (1973), 241-5; Fernández-Armesto, *Before Columbus,* 203-17.

100 Felipe Fernández-Armesto, *The Canary islands after the conquest. The making of a colonial society in the early sixteenth century* (Oxford, 1982).

faith.' Living among Christians, the converts will take up 'the mechanical arts and other means to life,' for until now they lack all knowledge of 'human industry.'[101] The puzzle of how to deal with the 'wild', unlettered Canary population was compounded by the fact that they belonged to no known religious category and had never had access, as had Muslims, Jews and arguably even Lithuanian pagans to the word of Christ. Just as they shed their Jews and most of their Muslims, the Catholic Monarchs acquired a non-Christian population whose status in Church law was no less debatable; once again, they supported moves for the conversion of the Canary peoples, but there was no attempt at mass coercion, largely for fear that this would only create even stiffer resistance.

Columbus' first voyage coincided with the conquest of Palma in the Canaries; his return coincided with Lugo's full-scale assault on Tenerife, which was conquered by 1496. The Portuguese were continuing their advance down the west coast of Africa towards the Congo and the Cape. Such expeditions to real places must have seemed more attractive propositions than the scheme Columbus was hawking around the Portuguese and Castilian courts; his estimate of costs was staggering (the final figure approaches two million *maravedís*), and his demand to be appointed Admiral of the Ocean Sea and governor-cum-viceroy of all he might discover was impudent in the extreme, not least since he insisted he was going to

---

101 Muldoon, *Popes, lawyers and infidels,* 119-25; on the inhabitants J. Mercer, *The Canary islanders. Their prehistory, conquest and survival* (London, 1980) is interesting but uneven.

discover new routes to Japan and the east Asian mainland. He also stood to profit handsomely from trade in
precious metals, gems and other goods that were obtained in the Indies. Without the protection of the royal
financier, of *converso* origin, Luis de Santangel, he would
have failed entirely; experts who were consulted about
his proposal were rightly convinced that he had seriously underestimated the circumference of the globe.[102]
Columbus' own conviction was perhaps strengthened by
rumours he had heard on earlier voyages in the Atlantic,
maybe as far away as Iceland, where memories of the
Viking voyages to Greenland and America lingered; the
possibility cannot be entirely excluded that Portuguese,
Breton, Basque, English and other sailors knew of the
existence of the coast of Labrador already, but such in-
formation was neither diffused nor exploited, except perhaps by fishermen in search of cod and halibut.[103] The
Castilian decision to support Columbus was a last-min-
ute, marginal one, and there was a strong suspicion that
money was being sent down the Atlantic plughole. That
others would have crossed the Atlantic in lieu is obvious
enough; the northerly expedition of the Italian John Cabot,
out of Bristol, reached Newfoundland in 1497.

On the other hand, it was only to be expected that a
Genoese sailor (for he was nothing else, and of rather

---

102 Felipe Fernández-Armesto, *Columbus* (2nd ed., Oxford, 1991);
Fernández-Armesto, *Before Columbus,* 251-2.

103 S.E. Morison, *The Portuguese voyages to America before 1500*
(Cambridge, MA, 1940); E. Carus-Wilson, *Medieval merchant
venturers* (London, 1967), 98-142.

modest origins[104]) would look to Castile and Portugal for patronage, since there was such a long history of Genoese links to both royal courts. Columbus' genius lay in his persistence, in his navigational skills and, paradoxically, in his refusal to believe what others, such as the publicist Amerigo Vespucci, were to show to be true: that he had arrived nowhere near Asia. The fruit of his obstinacy was a series of further expeditions which opened to view the major Caribbean islands and the coast of Venezuela, and which resulted in the first Spanish settlements on Hispaniola. Columbus was certain of divine guidance; he named his first discovery (generally believed to be what is now Watling Island) San Salvador, 'Holy Saviour', and his second expedition had a complement of missionary friars aboard. It is clear that the Catholic Monarchs were especially excited at the thought that new opportunities for the conversion of the Asian peoples had been created; in 1509 Ferdinand II looked back on past events and insisted that a major motive of the expeditions 'has always been and still is in these matters of the Indies to convert the Indians to our Holy Catholic Faith so that their souls may not be lost; thus it is necessary for them to be taught the truths of our religion without any force whatsoever.'

The debate which had flared over the status of the Canarian peoples was greatly extended after the Carib and Amerindian peoples came to light.[105] In a sense it has

104 Fernández-Armesto, *Columbus*, 1.

105 There is a growing literature here: see, e.g. A.R. Pagden, *The fall of natural man* (Cambridge, 1982); Muldoon, *Popes, lawyers and infidels*, 132-52; Fernández-Armesto, *Before Columbus*, 223-45.

been revived in the late twentieth century, with attempts to brand Columbus as a mass murderer who destroyed a paradise.[106] Moreover, Columbus is said not to have 'discovered' America, for its inhabitants had known for millennia that it was there; rather, he 'invaded' it. Since the issue is the European discovery of America this statement seems particularly futile. More serious is the accusation that the conquest of America resulted in the suppression of indigenous cultures: mass slaughter, the burning of Aztec libraries, the pillaging of treasuries, whose gold was melted down, the imposition of a new religion. Western diseases ravaged the Amerindians, as also the Guanches, though the traffic in germs went both ways, if it is true that syphilis first arrived in Europe soon after 1492. In fact, Spanish culture often achieved an extraordinary synthesis with native American cultures; Mexican Christianity was to preserve much of the old religion under the façade of Catholicism, and traditional art forms survived in the remarkable architectural style of many colonial buildings, not least churches. Most importantly, none of this really reflects on Columbus, who could not be persuaded to believe in the existence of a New World, and whose contact with its inhabitants was limited to some often unhappy encounters with the Carib islanders. Later, clearly, the attempts to exploit Amerindian labour under the *encomienda* system gave rise to serious abuses, visible already before the death of Ferdinand II in 1516. The crown certainly wanted to ensure that the native population was not enslaved, but it allowed labour services to be imposed on the Indians. The ruthless exploita-

---

106 This is the view of Kirkpatrick Sale, *The conquest of Paradise* (London, 1991).

tion of these obligations by Spanish landlords stimulated the attempts of Fray Bartolomé de las Casas to secure a better deal for the Indians; but greed tended to triumph.[107]

What is striking is how quickly the Catholic Monarchs moved to take advantage of their new acquisitions in the west, even while they still thought they were talking about Asia. Pope Alexander VI Borgia, a Spaniard, brokered the Treaty of Tordesillas of 1494 between Portugal and Castile which was intended to protect Portuguese rights in Africa, Madeira and the Azores (but not the Canaries) and to allow Castile hegemony over what was supposedly East Asia.[108] Under the final agreement the line dividing the Portuguese from the Castilian sphere of influence lay west of the eastern rim of south America, with the result that when, in 1500, the Portuguese captain Cabral touched land there he established a Portuguese claim to what was to become Brazil.

Finally, it is noticeable that it was Castile, not Castile and Aragon, that was the beneficiary. The Catalans, despite, or maybe because of, their long maritime tradition, were largely excluded from trade in the Canaries and America.[109] Not Barcelona nor Valencia, but Seville, with

---

107 J.H. Elliott, *The Old world and the New* (Cambridge, 1970).

108 L. Weckmann's theories in *Las Bulas alejandrinas de 1493 y la Teoría política del papado medieval* (Mexico City, 1949) are generally regarded as exaggerated; cf. Muldoon, *Popes, lawyers and infidels*, 55, though he too makes errors.

109 For what contact there was, see *XIII Congrés d'Historia de la Corona d'Aragó*, vol. 4 (Palma de Mallorca, 1989-90).

its sizeable Genoese community of shippers and financiers, was to be the base for westward-bound expeditions; unwittingly Columbus handed his Genoese compatriots a superb prize, the opportunity to service the America trade. The exclusion of the Catalans should not suggest that the Catholic Monarchs sought to discriminate against Catalan interests, still less that Catalan trade had gone into irreversible decline: it had not. In reality, Ferdinand was adhering to the strict separation of Castile from Aragon which was a central feature of his policy, and which was only breached by the activities of the Spanish Inquisition (of Aragonese descent). Aragon's interests continued to lie in trade eastwards to Italy and Sicily, and southwards to north-west Africa. Indeed, Ferdinand was even prepared to use Castilian resources to strengthen Aragon's hand in the Mediterranean. The continuing importance of these policies at the time of the discovery of America must now be examined.

V. Iberia, the Mediterranean
and the Catholic Monarchs

The intention here is not to provide a full account of the foreign policy of the Catholic Monarchs, but to concentrate on those issues which provide clues to their conception of the relationship between Castile and Aragon. Four promising approaches can be identified. The first is the problem of the succession to the Spanish thrones; the second is the relationship with the other Iberian kingdoms, Portugal and Navarre; the third and fourth are Spanish policies in north Africa and in southern Italy, areas of longstanding concern to the Crown of Aragon.

The failure of Ferdinand and Isabella to provide a surviving male heir to their crowns resulted in a succession of expedients to find a future king: the Infante John died in 1497. A Jewish view was that these problems were the judgment of God against the persecutors of Israel.[110] For a brief moment new hopes of a male succession arose out of the decision to create warmer ties with Portugal; King Manuel married Isabella's daughter of the same name, and in 1498 she gave birth to a son, Miguel, who was therefore heir to all of Castile, Aragon and Portugal. The personal union achieved by Ferdinand and Isabella was surely about to be deepened and extended with the eventual succession of a single ruler. But once again the prince failed to survive, dying in 1500. It now seemed likely that the succession would devolve on another daughter of the Catholic Monarchs, Juana, about whose sanity there were increasing doubts, and on her husband, the Flemish archduke Philip, whose knowledge of Spanish affairs was very limited. These difficulties were accentuated when Isabella died in 1504, leaving Ferdinand's status in Castile very uncertain; he had ruled in right of his wife, and her death should mark also the end of his reign. Moreover, he had made enough enemies at the Castilian court to make it unlikely that the nobility would support any attempt to hold on to the crown of Castile.

Ferdinand tried to make up for the loss of Castile by withdrawing to Aragon, and awaiting the arrival from

---

110 Joseph ha-Cohen, *Vale of Tears*, 68.

Flanders of Philip and Juana, who were set to become rulers of Castile. Ferdinand accordingly tried to ensure that his own patrimony, the lands of the Crown of Aragon, would have a native-born ruler once again. He chose a new bride, Germaine of Foix, who would, he hoped, produce a male heir to Aragon as well as some diplomatic advantages in his relations with France and Navarre. Once again a son was born, but lived only a short time. What is significant is that Ferdinand did not see a single succession to Castile and Aragon as his main priority. However, in the summer of 1506 the Treaty of Villafáfila between Philip and Ferdinand marked an attempt to secure a few remaining rights in Castile to Ferdinand, such as the mastership of the Military Orders and a half share in royal income from Caribbean trade. At least Ferdinand was able to show that he could not be totally excluded from Castilian politics; and the unexpected death of Philip late the same year, while Ferdinand was away in Naples, prompted Cisneros and his followers to summon Ferdinand back as regent. The alternative seemed to be a relapse into the divisiveness that had been rampant half a century before under Henry IV. The rights of Juana were easily set aside by making public her mental state. Castile thus fell into Ferdinand's hands by chance; and even so he had to reconcile himself to the eventual succession of yet another Flemish prince, Philip's son Charles of Habsburg (the future Emperor Charles V). Plans to bring Charles to Spain and to transform him into a Castilian Infante came to nothing.[111]

---

111 Elliott, *Imperial Spain,* 125-33; Ramsey, *Spain,* 290-318

Further evidence of Ferdinand's attitude to relations between Aragon and Castile can be found in his policy towards Navarre. This kingdom had for centuries been coveted by its Aragonese neighbours; in fact, Ferdinand's own father had recently ruled Navarre before succeeding Alfonso V on the throne of Aragon; Navarre had passed into the hands of the powerful and autonomous counts of Foix. By marrying into the house of Foix after the death of Isabella, Ferdinand acquired a contested claim to Navarre. Castilian influence in Navarre was certainly strong, as the suppression of the Navarrese Jews in 1498 reveals; but it was only in 1512 that Ferdinand was sufficiently free of Italian distractions to enforce his rights, by challenging the king of Navarre to grant Castilian armies access through the kingdom to France, with which Ferdinand was then at war. Navarrese refusal gave Ferdinand the excuse for a swift, clean occupation of nearly all the mountain state, followed a few months later by papal recognition of his claims. The commonly stated view that Ferdinand at once extended Castilian law to Navarre is incorrect; his first aim was to link it to Aragon, and it was only shortly before he died that he tied it to the Castilian crown, possibly in an attempt to placate his foes in Castile. Like any Aragonese king, he respected ancient autonomies, and Navarre retained its own *Cortes*, as well as possessing a *Diputación* (a permanent committee of the *Cortes*) on the Catalan model. Indeed, the chronicler Zurita believed that Ferdinand was afraid union with Aragon would prompt the Navarrese to claim further liberties similar to those of the Aragonese.[112] As a matter of fact, Ferdinand's victory was not com-

---

112 Elliott, *Imperial Spain*, 131-2; Ramsey, *Spain*, 315-7.

plete: a tiny trans-Pyrenean rump survived as a separate, French-dominated kingdom of Navarre.

The question of relations with Portugal has been addressed already; tension was generated by the Castilian-Aragonese marriage, by claims to the Canaries and eventually by Columbus' discoveries. The marriage negotiations of 1497 were thus a step in a new direction; but it is interesting to find that one of Castile's preconditions for the alliance was the expulsion of Portugal's Jews, many of whom were recent refugees from Spain. Even in diplomacy between the Iberian kingdoms, Isabella's unbending principles were not set aside.

Another area where Castile and Portugal competed was Morocco. The conquest of Ceuta by Portugal, in 1415, stimulated debate about which Iberian power was entitled to which part of a reconquered north Africa. Thus even before the fall of Granada such debates were far from theoretical; as well as past Castilian campaigns, there were traditional Catalan trading interests to consider in what are now Algeria and Tunisia. The collapse of al-Andalus was recognised as an epoch-making event; but it was by no means the end of the *reconquista*. Distinguished medieval commentators such as Ramón Llull (1232-1316) had argued that once Spain was in Christian hands, its rulers must press on across the Straits of Gibraltar. The distraction of wars in Italy wars slowed the African campaigns, but a significant start was made in 1496-7 when the duke of Medina Sidonia sent an army to take Melilla, which effectively marked the western edge of a Castilian sphere in Africa, with Portuguese rights assigned to the area beyond. Melilla, with one or two brief intervals, has remained part of Spain ever since. From 1505 onwards renewed campaigns, in which Cisneros took a leading part, resulted in the acquisition of Mers el-Kebir and of the important commercial centre of Oran (1509), of Bougie (1510), and of a line of cities extending as far east as Tripoli (captured in 1511). Most were placed under the Castilian flag, and seized with Castilian resources, but Tripoli was not unreasonably attached to the nearby Sicilian kingdom.[113] Ferdinand forced the Jews out of these territories too; they included many Spanish exiles.[114] The problem was that conquering the outer edge of the limitless expanse of Africa was not like conquering Spain: for one thing, the population consisted only of Muslims and Jews; for another, the further east the Spanish fleets moved, the nearer they came to the advancing Turkish armies which were shortly (1517) to overwhelm Egypt.

The Catholic Monarchs saw the expeditions as crusades, and Pope Alexander VI was generous with grants of crusade taxes. Yet the African conquests must also be seen as the fruit of centuries of Catalan-Aragonese ambition in the western Mediterranean, of which Ferdinand II of Aragon was now the standard bearer, even if it now proved easier to achieve results with Castilian armies. The basic conception of securing control of the prosperous ports of Morocco, Algeria and Tunisia, which had long served as termini for the gold caravans crossing the

---

113 A.C. Hess, *The forgotten frontier: a history of the sixteenth-century Ibero-African frontier* (Chicago, 1978); Elliott, *Imperial Spain*, 41-4; Ramsey, *Spain*, 232-7.

114 Joseph ha-Cohen, *Vale of Tears*, 74.

Sahara, went back centuries. It is possible too that the African conquests were thought necessary to secure the safety of the sea routes bringing Sicilian grain and other produce of the island kingdoms of the Crown of Aragon to the Spanish mainland.[115]

The other major concern of fifteenth-century Aragonese kings in the western Mediterranean was southern Italy. After seizing the area in the 1440's, Alfonso the Magnanimous bequeathed the kingdom of Naples to his cruel but able bastard son Ferrante I (1458-94). The separation of Naples from the Crown of Aragon did not deprive Ferrante of Aragonese help when he needed it; Aragonese and Castilian fleets helped see off the Turkish invaders who occupied Otranto, opposite the coast of Albania, in 1480-1. But the accession of Ferrante's son, the loathsome Alfonso II of Naples, a couple of years after the fall of Granada, coincided with the revival of grandiose French plans for the assertion of the rights of the house of Anjou to the kingdom of Naples. Under Alfonso the Magnanimous and Ferrante, these claims had resulted in attempts by Duke René of Anjou, Lorraine and Provence to seize Naples; but his rights had now devolved on a youthful, romantic, politically blind French king, Charles VIII. The history of the French invasions of Italy does not need to be repeated here.[116] What is important is

---

115 Braudel, *Mediterranean,* i.117-18.

116 Unfortunately there is no modern account of the later Aragonese kings of Naples; for an outline, see Bentley, *Politics and culture.* On Charles VIII see Y. Labande-Maillfert, *Charles VIII et son milieu. La jeunesse au pouvoir (1470-1495)* (Paris, 1975); Y. Labande-Maillfert, *Charles VIII. Le vouloir et la destiné* (Paris, 1986); A. Denis, *Charles VIII et les italiens: histoire et mythe* (Geneva, 1979).

that Ferdinand exploited the weakness of his Aragonese
kinsmen, the kings of Naples, to assert his own claims
as well. One important gain was the lost Catalan counties of Roussillon and Cerdagne, which had been occupied by Louis XI of France in 1463, during the Catalan
civil war. Thirty years later, after endless diplomatic ini-
tiatives (including an Anglo-Aragonese alliance against
France) Ferdinand won back the two counties peacefully
because Charles VIII was too obsessed with his Italian
plans to care about retaining them.[117] Charles briefly occupied Naples; but by 1497, when an agreement was
signed at Alcala de Henares between the French and the
Spaniards, Ferdinand had manoeuvred Charles VIII into
a position where the French agreed to the partition of
southern Italy. At first Ferdinand of Aragon was to re-
ceive only Calabria, the toe of Italy adjoining his existing possession of Sicily; but the Treaty of Granada with
King Louis XII of France (1500) promised the valuable
south-east of Italy, Apulia, as well. When in the next
few years the French attempted to assert their claims, the
Aragonese literally stood in their way; by the end of
1503 southern Italy was in Aragonese hands - but the
hands of Ferdinand and not of the local Aragonese dynasty, whose last ruler, the likeable Federigo, had been
pensioned off. Among the victims of the war were, as
has been seen, the south Italian Jews, most of whom
who were eventually ordered to leave the kingdom.

It was quite patently old Aragonese interests that drew
the Spaniards to Italy under Ferdinand II. Ferdinand him-

---

117 J. Calmette, *La question des Pyrénées et la Marche d'Espagne
au Moyen Age* (9th ed., Paris, 1947).

self travelled to Naples during the period when he was excluded from the government of Castile; his actions are in many respects a replay of those of his predecessor Alfonso the Magnanimous. Like Alfonso, who had harboured ambitions of influence in Castile (though he never gained its crown), Ferdinand saw his Castilian schemes collapse and turned eastward to reactivate Aragonese claims in southern Italy. These were of special importance at a time when Turkish advances threatened the central Mediterranean. Ferdinand's use of Castilian fleets and commanders is arguably neither here nor there; if anything, it was a brilliant way to make Castile pay for Aragon's needs. He was fighting for yet another personal crown, not for a Spanish empire in Italy. It is possible that he believed his policies would stimulate the recovery of Barcelona's trade with Italy, which had been so intense under Alfonso V; and this would strengthen royal finances in Catalonia and in Naples. The timing was right; population growth in the late fifteenth century led to a revival of demand for the raw materials and foodstuffs of southern Italy and Sicily. Finally, Ferdinand was bound to give his Italian ambitions priority over the Castilian conquests in the New World, since his own position in Castile was relatively precarious and since it was still far from clear what America could offer and how the colonies were to be managed. Traditional policies might be expected to produce reasonably predictable results.

In other words, Ferdinand was guided less by a vision of the future than by a knowledge of the past. And as for Isabella, she was guided by a vision of the hereafter more than by one of the here and now. The Catholic Monarchs neither aimed at nor achieved the unification of Spain; they did not even achieve its Christianisation, though for Isabella at any rate this was the highest of objectives.

FURTHER READING

The intention here is to concentrate on recent literature, mainly in English, that will lead a stage deeper into the problems of the Catholic Monarchs. References to a number of other specialised books and articles, including some in French, Castilian, Catalan, Portuguese and Italian, will be found in the notes.

General surveys (including foreign policy)

J.H. Elliott, *Imperial Spain 1469-1716* (London, 1963) is a splendidly readable account of the period, but even the lengthy account of the fifteenth century is written very much from a sixteenth-century perspective, and this brilliant book now needs to be updated. The same perspective bedevils the fine survey of Henry Kamen, *Spain 1469-1714. A society of conflict* (2nd ed., London, 1991; the section on Ferdinand and Isabella seems unchanged since the first edition of 1983). J.N. Hillgarth, *The Spanish Kingdoms,* vol. 2, *Castilian Hegemony, 1410-1516* (Oxford, 1978) is essential and encyclopaedic, and does not suffer from the same fault. *Spain in the fifteenth century 1369-1500* (London, 1972) consists of a valuable series of articles, several by Spanish historians, edited by J.R.L. Highfield. From the medieval end there is an excellent survey by A. Mackay, *Spain in the Middle Ages. From frontier to empire, 1100-1500* (London, 1977); see too T.N. Bisson, *The medieval Crown of Aragon. A short history* (Oxford, 1985). The Aragonese background, in Spain, Italy and Sicily, is accessible in the works of Alan Ryder: 'The evolution of imperial government in Naples under Alfonso V,' in J.R.L. Highfield, B. Smalley (eds) *Europe in the late Middle Ages* (London, 1965), 332-57; *Alfonso the Magnanimous* (Oxford, 1990); *The Kingdom of Naples under Alfonso the Magnanimous* (Oxford, 1975). For an unusual approach, see J.F. Ramsey, *Spain: the rise of the first World Power* (Alabama, 1973). On internal affairs, see M. Lunenfeld, *The Council of the Santa Hermandad* (Miami, 1970), and the same author's *Keepers of the City. The corregidores of Isabella of Castile (1474-1504)* (Cambridge, 1988); see also L.P. Wright, 'The military orders in sixteenth and seventeenth-century Spanish society,' *Past and Present,* no.43 (1969); J.R.L. Highfield, 'The Catholic Kings and the titled nobility of Castile', in Hale, Highfield, Smalley (eds) *Europe in the late Middle Ages* (above), 358-85, a fine article that nonetheless begins by talking of a 'reign which saw Spain a united country.' There is also a biography by Felipe Fernández-Armesto, *Ferdinand and Isabella* (London, 1975). R. Boase, *The Troubadour Revival. A study of social change and traditionalism in late medieval Spain* (London, 1978) has considerable bearing on the issues raised here.

The fall of Granada

L.P. Harvey, *Islamic Spain 1250-1500* (Chicago, 1991) is especially strong on political and religious problems, and looks both at Granada and at the *mudéjares*; much of the other literature on Moorish Spain tails off after 1250. R. Arié, *L'Espagne musulmane au temps des*

Nasrides (2nd ed., Paris, 1990) is a major study of Granada. Mark Meyerson's outstanding *The Muslims of Valencia in the age of Fernando and Isabel* (Berkeley/Los Angeles, 1991) breaks new ground; for the later history of the Valencian Muslims see now S. Haliczer, *Inquisition and society in the Kingdom of Valencia, 1478-1834* (Berkeley/ Los Angeles, 1990). Anwar G. Chejne, *Islam and the West: the Moriscos. A cultural and social history* (Albany, NY, 1983) mixes up material from before and after 1492, though the details are interesting.

The expulsion of the Jews

Outline histories of the Jews in later medieval Spain include Y. Baer, *A History of the Jews in Christian Spain*, vol. 2, *From the fourteenth century to the Expulsion* (Philadelphia, 1961) and, more generally, L. Suarez Fernández, *Les juifs espagnols au Moyen Age* (Paris, 1983) and M. Kriegel, *Les juifs à la fin du Moyen Age dans l'Europe méditerranéenne* (Paris, 1979); see also Hillgarth, *The Spanish Kingdoms* (above). Valuable articles include J.H. Edwards, 'Religious belief and social conformity: the *converso* problem in late medieval Córdoba,' *Transactions of the Royal Historical Society,* ser. 5, xxxi (1981); A. Mackay, 'Popular movements and pogroms in fifteenth-century Castile,' *Past and Present,* no. 55 (1972), 33-67; A. Mackay 'The Hispanic-Converso predicament,' *Transactions of the Royal Historical Society,* ser. 5, xxxv (1985), 159-79. Mackay's articles are now available collected in a single volume, *Society, economy and religion in late medieval Castile* (London, 1987). A special case study is B. Gampel, *The last Jews on Iberian soil. Navarrese Jewry 1497/8* (Berkeley/Los Angeles, 1989). A popular account of Spanish Jewry is C. Raphael, *The road from Babylon* (London, 1985, new ed. as *The Sephardi story*, London, 1991); see also B. Leroy, *L'aventure séfarade. De la péninsule ibérique á la diaspora* (Paris, 1986), both of which go beyond 1492; and, for the Sephardim in the Mediterranean, see R. Patai, *The vanished worlds of Jewry* (London, 1981), and, more seriously, R. Barnett and W. Schwab (eds), *The Sephardi Heritage*, vol. 2, *The western Sephardim* (Gibraltar, 1990). There is much of value in J. Israel, *European Jewry in the age of Mercantilism 1550-1750* (2nd ed., Oxford, 1989); see also John Edwards, *The Jews in Christian Europe, 1400-1700* (London, 1988). The books of Cecil Roth, including *A History of the Marranos* (Philadelphia, 1932), and *A History of the Jews in Italy* (Philadelphia, 1946), are very dated in approach, but often cover ground not surveyed elsewhere; see now H. Kamen's excellent studies of the Inquisition: *Inquisition and society in Spain in the sixteenth and seventeenth centuries* (London, 1985), largely replacing his *The Spanish Inquisition* (London, 1965), adding W. Monter, *Frontiers of heresy. The Spanish Inquisition from the Basque lands to Sicily* (Cambridge, 1990), and the study by S. Haliczer noted above; K. Moore, *Those of the Street. The Catholic-Jews of Mallorca* (Notre Dame, IN, 1976) is an interesting study of identity under persecution, though not typical of all Spain. For some radical ideas about the expulsion and its survivors, see B. Netanyahu, *The Marranos of Spain, from the late fourteenth to the early sixteenth century according to contemporary Hebrew sources* (2nd ed., New York, 1973); compare H. Kamen, 'The Mediterranean and the expulsion of Spanish Jews in 1492,' *Past and Present*, no. 119 (1988).

Atlantic exploration

The literature is endless, and of very variable worth. A very good starting point is Felipe Fernández-Armesto, *Before Columbus. Exploration and colonisation from the Mediterranean to the Atlantic, 1229-1492* (London, 1987), which is lively on the Catalan and Genoese background; compare the more materialistic approach of P. Chaunu, *European expansion in the later Middle Ages* (Amsterdam, 1979). On the early Atlantic settlements, see C. Verlinden, *The beginnings of modern colonization* (Ithaca, NY, 1970), and Felipe Fernández-Armesto, *The Canary Islands after the Conquest. The making of a colonial society in the early sixteenth century* (Oxford, 1982). J. Muldoon, *Popes, lawyers and infidels. The Church and the non-Christian world 1250-1500* (Liverpool, 1979) addresses the problem of the treatment of pagan peoples. Early links between Genoa, Portugal and the Atlantic are explored in B.W. Diffie, *Prelude to Empire. Portugal overseas before Henry the Navigator* (Nebraska, 1960). For Portuguese and Castilian exploration, and for Genoese connections, see G.V. Scammell, *The World encompassed. The first European maritime empires, c.800-1650* (London, 1981), which makes the strange error of omitting the Catalans, and the works of J.H. Parry, notably *The Discovery of the Sea* (London, 1975). For Henry the Navigator, the sensible approach is that in two pamphlets by P.E. Russell, *Prince Henry the Navigator* (London, 1960), and *Prince Henry the Navigator: the rise and fall of a culture hero* (Oxford, 1984). Columbus has had yet more biographers; many questions are analysed in relentless detail in P.E. Taviani's monumental *Christopher Columbus. The grand design* (London, 1985); but the major biography remains that of S.E. Morison, *Admiral of the Ocean Sea,* 2 vols (Cambridge, MA, 1942), to which should be added Admiral Morison's *The European Discovery of America: the southern voyages* (Oxford, 1974). A welcome short biography is that of the prolific Felipe Fernández-Armesto, *Columbus* (Oxford, 1991, recasting an earlier life by the same author).